"*Your Second Chapter* takes you by the hand and leads [illegible] and happier future. Vera Holloway has a [illegible] onal health and making it easy to unde[illegible] her framework step-by-step. This is the b[illegible] ad."

—*Alli Worthington, bestselling author and business coach*

"Every one of us are given something in the first chapter of our lives that we wished was different. Vera inspires us all to grab the opportunity given by Christ to write ourselves a different story. *Your Second Chapter* remains active within us far beyond the last page. We were privileged to host several semesters of Vera's BFA curriculum at our church. The results for the attendees were lifechanging. If you want to leverage the pain of yesterday into a different tomorrow, this is your book."

—*Keesha and Josh Melancon, pastors of House of Prayer Church*

"The emotional scars and mental wounds of trauma oftentimes mimic physical injuries such as those inflicted during strenuous athletic training. In *Your Second Chapter*, Vera coaches the reader in Biblical, functional, and applicable ways that lead to endurance, perseverance, and steadfastness in the race towards emotional stability and the fight for mental wellness. Let this book be your guide for strengthening the emotional and mental muscles you need to get your life's win."

—*Tina Gilfour Rumore, Licensed Professional Counselor*

"The mental health emergency our world is currently facing now has a great resource for help and healing. Vera created a mental health guide that is both engaging and empowering and put it in within reach of everyone in need of a do over. *Your Second Chapter* walks readers through the process of getting unstuck! Whether experiencing a crisis yourself or supporting someone who has, I think you'll find this book the most useful tool in the box."

—April Snook, founder of JesusPeopleCo
and @HowToDoLifeWithGod,
Bridges Safehouse board member

"Vera Holloway is going to change your life! Her compassion and heart will help you see the value in yourself as God intended you to be. A must read!"

—Leah Silverii, author and Vera's friend

"Vera's insight into wholeness and healing is second to none. In addition to her incredible experience and training she is battle-tested having faced her own beauty for ashes story. For anyone ready to get unstuck, and gain the clarity needed to begin your second chapter in life with healing, peace and purpose this book is for you! *Your Second Chapter* will be a helpful tool in our crisis center to help our clients move from an unhealthy cycle of stuck to liberty and beauty."

—Maria Braud, executive director of Hope Restored PRC

Your Second Chapter

Moving from Stuck to
Peace, Purpose, and Productivity

Vera Holloway

Your Second Chapter: Moving from Stuck to Peace, Purpose, and Productivity

First Edition, February 2022

Cover Design by Dar Albert
Cover Photos by Hannah Gros, hannahgrosphotos.com
Formatting by Dallas Hodge, dalhodge56@gmail.com
Page Design Elements by Alyssa G. Bruce
Interior Photos by Jordan Roebuck

Published by *The People Company*, Thibodaux, LA 70301
thepeoplecompany.org

This work is cataloged in the Library of Congress.
ISBN: 978-1-73373682-4 (hardback)
ISBN: 978-1-7337368-3-1 (paperback)

To my Clients and my BFA students.
Your bravery inspires me.
What an honor to be trusted with your vulnerability.
You are my greatest teacher.

Table of Contents

How This Book Came To Be

In 2017, my eighth year of full-time mental health work, I was pursuing my doctorate in counseling, all while holding up my end as a partner of a three-year-old company specializing in applied behavior analysis. As a result, I had multiple irons in the fire, both professionally and personally. I was reading everything I could get my hands on related to trauma as part of my early dissertation work, and my clients were begging me for a book.

In addition to what I already had going on, many others wanted to join my client list, but I had no opening. When was I going to write a book? I could barely catch my breath, let alone take on another project. I needed something to open up.

The people pleaser in me has a natural inclination toward accommodating everyone. And the mental health needs of the people contacting my office for appointments pulled at my heart.

Then the Lord started speaking to me about my options. I could continue to see thirty to forty clients a week and run myself ragged and live full of guilt. I could teach, again limiting my reach. Or I could put something out there based on what I was studying and what the Lord was teaching me that would make my reach limitless.

My first effort became a ten-week curriculum called Beauty From Ashes (BFA). I thought this might help a few dozen women. So, starting with a group of eight women at a local church, I launched the curriculum. It took off like a fire on dry kindling.

Immediately after that first ten-week session ended, I began another one. Every session included facilitators I previously trained to guide attendees through small group time. The response was astounding and instantly required two ten-week sessions per year. We had to cap each ten-week session at one hundred women. I went to other areas and trained women as facilitators, coaching them through the program. I also had Facebook groups from the east and west coasts of the United States joining each week.

This book, *Your Second Chapter*, is a compilation of the session handouts and what I taught each week. The stories from clients and BFA attendees are true, but the names and identifying details are changed to provide anonymity. In some cases, the stories are compilations of several clients and BFA graduates. And, of course, some of these stories are about me.

I pray readers find hope and healing using this book, as did hundreds of women and men. Remember, this book is not a psychological diagnostic tool and should not be used as such. Instead, it's a tool for self-evaluation, one designed to promote inner healing. And it's explicitly intended to open your understanding of what God will do for you when you let him.

How To Use This Book

A letter from the author

As I sit here and write this letter to you, the reader, Hurricane Ida has just blown through my bayou community in southeast Louisiana. It's like ground zero all over again. Exactly sixteen years to the day of Hurricane Katrina, we found ourselves bracing for the monster storm named Ida. I have lived through many hurricanes in my lifetime, but this one was different.

It took me by surprise and took our bayou community by surprise too. The storm approaching was no surprise, but the intensity and violence were on a level never before experienced here. Meteorologists reported Ida as the fifth most powerful storm to hit the United States with a wind speed faster than Hurricane Katrina at landfall.

In case you don't understand what that means, let me explain. Warm waters, such as those found in the Gulf of Mexico, intensify a storm. Typically making landfall causes a storm to lose intensity because it loses the thing that feeds it. However, Ida did not lose intensity. Instead, she maintained her strength in what is known as the "brown ocean effect." Ida's own storm surge, the rise of water above the normal tide, and floodwater acted like an "ocean" and continued to release heat into the storm's center, helping her maintain her intensity. Consequently, five hours after Ida came onshore, her winds were still at Category 4 level with 130 m.p.h. winds. Definitely not an ordinary storm.

I want you to mark the above paragraph. Why? Because everything in nature has a corresponding human correlation. And I will refer back to the storm analogy later in this book.

"But ask the animals, and they will teach you, or the birds in the sky, and they will tell you; or speak to the earth, and it will teach you, or let the fish in the sea inform you" (Job 12:7–8).

After the storm passed, I looked at my husband and told him, "I have had enough hurricane trauma for a lifetime! Get me out of here!". With life being on pause—no electricity, schools, and businesses closed; everyone assessing the damages and beginning the long journey of cleanup and rebuilding—I began to think about what living through storms, physically and mentally, has taught me. I sure do have some experience. My first thought was:

"We are in the same storm, but not the same boat. So, let's stop the comparison and start giving compassion."

What do I mean by that? The storm is the same. We understand and recognize what a storm feels like in the physical, but we process it differently. The way we seek safety is different. Even what we consider as safety is different! Some people have a good boat to get them to a safe place, some may have a yacht, and some only have a life preserver. Some are trying to swim through the storm with no safety device, and sadly some are drowning in the raging waters.

Same storm, but different perspectives. Different situations. You can't compare trauma stories. One is not more profound than the other. It was a storm, no doubt, and you share in that understanding, but how you handle the waters of that trauma is different based on what resources you had around you.

I recommend you take this book as a personal lifeline, but I also want you to share this lifeline. Since we have all been through a storm of some sort—we can understand how important it is to extend a lifeline in a time of need.

This book may absolutely be for you and come at just the right time, but if not, share this with someone. Read this book and learn, you may think you don't need it now and you may not, but you may find that it helps you become a stronger and healthier person even though you were never "stuck." It will definitely put you in a better position to help a friend or family member by offering support and love even though you are not in the same boat. The material in this book is for all women (and men too!).

I am with you in this. I have been through many storms and now I'm standing on the other side extending my hand to bring others into their second chapter!

So, let's make room for that second chapter. Let's do the hard work. Allow me to guide you in actually writing your second chapter. This book is interactive. It will take some time, but you owe it to yourself or your loved ones to do it! So, let's toast to our second chapter being full of peace, purpose, and productivity. Cheers, my girls!

Vera

Introduction

Vera Holloway

The day was beautiful. Perfect weather for an outdoor wedding. Not too hot. Not too cold. Which in south Louisiana is a small miracle. Under those ancient oak trees, the white chairs, set in patterns designed to mark out a pathway for the bride, gave the best view for the guests. The chairs looked pretty against the green of the lawn. But I wasn't taking in any of that. Instead, I was staring at that massive oak door in front of me.

The property manager of the idyllic plantation, a Frenchwoman with pale skin and shoulder length blonde hair, was standing beside me. But, aside from this pleasant lady, a stranger, I was alone.

I could feel her eyes on me. And I wondered what she was thinking. I hoped she didn't pity me. I don't think I could have stood it, this stranger showing more compassion and support for me than my parents had.

She gave me a final look, a final cue, and opened the door for me to walk down the aisle. I began walking what felt like a never-ending journey past a sea of staring eyes.

Yes, I know this is what one does when a bride is walking down the aisle. All the guests take in the bride's beauty, dress, and emotions—it's the reason they attend—these friends and family of the bride and groom. Except, I suspected they had heard the rumors, and I wondered how many had shown up to see if what they heard was true.

It was my wedding day, and I focused on the moment and disassociated from this latest letdown. The avoider in me was good at that.

Abandoned once again, but this time I was going to own it like a boss. So, head held high, eyes focused forward, I stepped out.

The decision to not reject those who rejected me calmed my mind. The peace of accepting what I could not change at that moment, and the love of my life, Seth, got me through that momentous day.

But it wouldn't be long before the stain left from abandonment would pop up again and again disguised as something else.

Traumas always do. Until they don't.

Chapter One

Identifying Stuck

Phase One
Abandonment

"Abandonment is the real slayer of the soul"
—Marnie C. Ferree

Walking alone down the aisle was not my first encounter with abandonment, but it was perhaps one of the most devastating of my adult life. You may wonder what I did wrong to find myself without the support of those that matter the most on a day that mattered the most.

Well, I wondered that as well. You see, it wasn't something I had done wrong but something I thought was right. For once in my life, I wasn't club-hopping or excessively drinking, both of which led to things I would come to regret. I had a newfound faith in Jesus and a guy who put God first in everything. I was, for the first time, living differently. I wasn't living in a constant state of repentance because I felt guilty for past decisions. I expected my parents to be happy for me. The sticking point for them? My newfound faith and my guy were in a religion other than the faith of my parents.

My adoptive father, who raised me and took on the responsibility of a child not biologically his to the point of legally adopting me, refused to attend my wedding. My mom and my two younger brothers, both minors at the time, were not allowed to attend either, though my mother stated that it was her choice not to attend. Tradition and religious rules are what my parents used as the reasons they were not supporting me that day.

Until the very day of my wedding, I hoped my dad would relent and attend, or at least allow my brothers to be there. But, instead, my parents took my younger brothers out of town for the weekend.

My parents told me attending my Christian ceremony would be sinful, and they would have to account for such decisions at the end of this life. Yes, we were all Christians at the end of the day, but my ceremony and vows performed outside the umbrella of my childhood religion caused my parents to believe I was living in sin.

After many tough conversations ending in disagreement every time, I decided to continue loving and respecting them. Although I was hurt, I humbled myself and chose not to speak ill of my parents. Talk about hard.

Living in a small town didn't help because word got around fast. "Vera is getting married, and her parents are not going because it wasn't in the church they wanted!" I felt so much was stolen from me on that day.

But my other options were anger, bitterness, resentment, and disrespect. How would that benefit me or anyone else? Oh, but if I could have only known what was to come from the ashes of my brokenness perhaps it would have been easier to bear.

Making their absence more glaring was that all of my extended family on both sides attended. And they all were of the same faith as my parents. In addition, many of my high school and college friends were of the same faith as my parents and also attended. It just didn't make much sense to the outsider, and it was confusing for me. My parents' choices didn't seem Christlike in the least, but to not be bitter, I knew I had to respond opposite to what my feelings were demanding.

John, my Austrian born, larger than life, biological father, had signed away his rights as my parent when I was seven years old. He unexpectedly contacted me before my wedding and offered money for wedding expenses—my parents had withdrawn financial support as well as emotional support. John stated straight out that he knew he had no right to the honor but would walk me down the aisle if I wished. I refused. The man that I always envisioned walking me down the aisle wasn't going to be there, so surely, I wasn't going to let John step in for the day. No, it didn't work that way.

Though I didn't fully recognize what John leaving me meant—that revelation came years later—I felt no desire to have him rush in and fix things. I was the woman who took care of herself, solved her problems with grit and determination. Sort of. Mostly. Temporarily. Ugh, what a mess!

Abandonment is complex and often difficult to identify, unlike physical, emotional, sexual, spiritual, and financial abuse.

Unfortunately, most people do not recognize they were abandoned until much later in life. How do you know you missed something when you've never had it, right?

One of my BFA students, Nikki, relays her experience of abandonment like this:

> *"She* [her mother] *meets my dad—and supposedly he had left his wife—he was separated, with hopes to marry my mom. And my mom got pregnant with me. But he never left his wife. So, my mom, to protect me and him, I guess,*

> *I don't know who she was protecting, moved away while pregnant so no one would know that she was pregnant. A couple of weeks after giving birth, she came back, handed me over to my grandmother, and said 'Here, this one is yours.' So my grandmother raised me.*
>
> *I was pretty much fully aware of my illegitimacy because my siblings lived with my mom and stepdad, but I could only go visit every now and then.*
>
> *I guess it's like you're on the outside looking in. Wishing you could be in that fold with the other kids, but you have to go* [back] *with your grandmother.*
>
> *My grandmother was a wonderful, praying Christian woman who raised me pretty much like the little girl on Madea Goes to Jail when Madea finds the little girl and dresses her from head to toe. That little girl was me."*

In many ways, the effects of abandonment are more profound than the consequences of abuse. The wounds are deeper, more camouflaged, and more challenging to heal.

The pain of abandonment is part of the human condition.[1] It's one consequence of the original sin committed in the garden of Eden, which separated humans from God. Thus, we all know some form of abandonment.

1 ***No Stones: Women Redeemed From Sexual Addiction*** Ferree, Marnie C., IVP Books, 2010

Tracking Abandonment

Abandonment issues find their roots in early childhood experiences. The most common ones are listed—emotional, physical, sexual, spiritual, and financial—use the checkboxes[2] for objective personal evaluation, not as a knife to slice open a sensitive scar. Remember that a look at the past is not meant to pin you in places you don't want to stay. We do not get healing from things we refuse to acknowledge. God is with you. He said he will never leave you. You can do this.

2 The **Wounds of Abandonment** checklists were initially based on a chart of symptoms in *No Stones* by Marnie C. Ferree and owe their origin to Dr. Mark Laaser, *Healing the Wounds of Sexual Addiction*, Zondervan, 2004, with further additions by Vera Holloway.

Wounds of Abandonment

FINANCIAL

- ☐ left to provide for yourself prior to adulthood financially
- ☐ responsible to financially support siblings or parents before adulthood
- ☐ lack of healthy information and modeling of sound financial choices
- ☐ death of a spouse left the remaining spouse to struggle financially

EMOTIONAL

- ☐ not listening
- ☐ no caring or nurturing
- ☐ no expression of affection

PHYSICAL

- ☐ being left alone, i.e., death of a parent/sibling, divorce, a parent being physically or mentally absent for long periods
- ☐ inadequate food, shelter, or clothing
- ☐ no modeling of physical self-care

SEXUAL

- ☐ no intimacy modeled
- ☐ lack of healthy information about sex

SPIRITUAL

- ☐ no spirituality modeled by an adult
- ☐ lack of spiritual discipline

Emotional Abandonment

It is possible to grow up and have a parent, or both parents, physically present but emotionally unavailable. During your childhood, your parents may have been emotionally absent. Some parents lack the skills and experience to nurture a child emotionally. They didn't learn in their own families of origin how to emotionally connect in relationships.

Beth Moore's reference to a parent's failure to nurture as "a hand withheld"[3] is a powerful description of what happens when withholding an emotional connection occurs. Suppose you identify with some of the descriptions of emotional abandonment listed in the previous checklist. In that case, you may have struggled in the past, or even possibly currently, with having secure attachments with others, particularly in romantic relationships.

Financial Abandonment

Some people may see financial abandonment as a subtype of a physical abandonment, but I have given it its own category because sometimes people experience financial abandonment without physical abandonment. Sadly, many experience both physical and financial abandonment simultaneously.

3 Beth Moore https://www.lproof.org/

The most common areas for financial abandonment are divorce, custody, and domestic violence cases, but that doesn't mean there are not many other scenarios where this happens. I will spend some time discussing financial abuse, which is different from financial abandonment.

What does financial abandonment look like? It looks like a parent, caregiver, or spouse who neglects financial obligations and responsibilities or doesn't maintain consistent employment. This lack of financial responsibility puts everyone in the family in jeopardy, causing undue stress as the family struggles to have basic necessities such as food, clothes, and a safe living environment.

In divorce and custody situations, we can sometimes see a spouse or parent stop providing financially for a minor child's care or an estranged spouse's medical or housing needs. They abandon them not only physically but also financially. I experienced this as a little girl when my biological father left and divorced my mother—he physically abandoned us, seeking no regular custody visitation schedule, and financially abandoned us.

My mother was not the primary income provider, so she moved closer to her family seeking help to care for my twin sister and me, and then began the process of starting over with no monthly child support payments from my father. Did she make it? Did she pull out of it? Yes, she did. But the burden of providing for us rested solely on her. She did a fabulous job, along with our extended family, to ensure my sister and I didn't know we were going without or even struggling. Looking back now, as an adult, I am amazed at how she made it work! Sadly, this is still a common occurrence; else, there would be no need for child support laws.

Sometimes the family's financial status is affected by the death or long-term illness of the family's primary income earner. This abandonment, though not deliberate, is no less traumatic to the family. One spouse dies and leaves the remaining spouse and children struggling to make ends meet. Or an unexpected illness of a parent or child creates a financial struggle that redefines life for everyone in the family.

Another example of financial abandonment is growing up in a home where healthy financial decisions are not modeled and taught. You don't have to grow up with a lot of money to learn sound principles of money, but solid financial decision-making needs to be modeled and taught. If your parents or caregivers didn't model this for you—it's important to find a mentor, read books, and do whatever you can to break that cycle.

We don't need to earn six figures to learn how to live within our means. Excessive spending in areas that are not necessary, poor money management, spending more money than is brought in monthly, excessive credit card debt are all behaviors typically linked to poor financial modeling in childhood.

If you grew up hearing money spoken about negatively or provisions were scarce, you may have learned that finances were something to be feared. Maybe you think that financial struggle is your destiny because your parents financially struggled.

Death and tragedy can result in financial abandonment as well. This type doesn't happen purposely but is a by-product of trauma. The death of a parent may cause the child to grow up with an unstable financial upbringing. The fears associated with that can produce a "never enough" mentality and a tendency toward hoarding.

Physical Abandonment

Physical abandonment takes many forms. The death of a parent is one form of physical abandonment. Divorce, the absence of parents due to work-related travel or military service, and the physically present parent who is mentally unavailable due to mental or physical illness are other examples.

One often thinks of a parent walking out of a child's life as physical abandonment, but there are other forms of physical abandonment. The loss of a close friendship, the death of a sibling, or an intimate partner walking out are all examples of physical abandonment. The circumstances are different but the abandonment remains the same.

Sometimes for genuine financial reasons, parents must work at jobs that require time away from home often. However, it's important to note that just because physical abandonment is innocent doesn't mean it won't negatively impact.

Sexual Abandonment

Sexual abandonment may seem odd in light of our overly sexualized culture. Our culture gives plenty of attention to sex, but sadly most parents do not! Few churches address sexuality in healthy ways either.

Many parents are uncomfortable talking about sex, even about the most basic biology concepts related to puberty and body changes. Parents are uncomfortable talking to their kids about sex because no one discussed sex with them when they were children.

Silence about sex is not healthy. Many Christians falsely believe that providing knowledge to their teens about sex somehow signals that they approve of their teens' sexual activity. The latest research indicates the exact opposite.

Those who are best informed are best able to make responsible decisions. They have less need to experiment. They have a safe place to talk about sexual temptations, which helps to lessen the temptation.

Evaluating where our information and ideas about sex originated helps us understand why we have hang-ups about sex. So, where did you get most of your knowledge about sex? Write out your thoughts here.

Our original ideas about sex, if erroneous, need to change if we hope to end an unhealthy cycle before our children suffer as we did. Are you comfortable talking to your kids about sex, or does it make you as nervous as a turkey the week of Thanksgiving? Evaluate your feelings about this so that you are aware of where you need guidance concerning this area when you get to Chapter Two.

Don't perpetuate the mistakes that were made with you by repeating past generational problems. You have the power to work along with the Holy Spirit to end past toxic familial structures. It stops with you!

Spiritual Abandonment

Spiritual development is impaired when you haven't received modeling or instruction. For example, perhaps you weren't taught the importance of values like honesty, integrity, generosity, or service.

Less recognizable is the spiritual abandonment that can occur even in a religiously devout home. Perhaps you went to church every time the doors were open. Maybe you had plenty of religious experiences but had no teaching about a genuine relationship with God.

The demand for compliance and strict rule-following rather than biblical truths modeled by loving, nurturing parents and guardians disconnects a child from the bridge of spiritual understanding intended to lead them to a personal spiritual experience as they mature.

Phase Two

Abuse

"Overcoming abuse doesn't just happen,
It takes positive steps every day.
Let today be the day you start to move forward."
— Assunta Harris

If you have personally experienced or witnessed abuse in your family, you have personally been harmed. Being unable to protect yourself or a loved one is traumatic. Abuse places tremendous guilt on the abused even though they are not the ones at fault.

We do no one a favor by taking on guilt that is not ours to own.

"Recognizing misplaced guilt is important to your healing and moving toward positive and permanent change."

Reread the previous sentence. It is an important truth.

The late Dr. Mark Laaser, the founder of Faithful and True, states that there are four types of abuse and refers to them as "invasion trauma."[4] The four types are emotional, physical, sexual, and spiritual. I go a step further and add financial abuse also. On the next page, you will see a checkbox for each type of trauma. Take some time and read through this list. Check the boxes that have happened to you or that you have witnessed firsthand happening to someone else.

4 https://integrityrestored.com/abuse-and-pornography-addiction/, The **Wounds of Abuse** chart was originally taken from the book No Stones by Marnie C. Ferree. Ferree stated she pulled the chart from the works of Dr. Mark Laaser, *Healing the Wounds of Sexual Addiction*, Zondervan, 2004.

Wounds of Abuse

FINANCIAL

- ☐ forbidding you to work, refusing to work themselves
- ☐ sabotaging your work, employment, or advancement opportunities
- ☐ controlling how money is spent:
- ☐ withholding or restricting your access, excluding you from financial decisions.
- ☐ hiding from you: assets, transactions, spending
- ☐ theft: using your identity (i.e., your social security number to obtain credit,
- ☐ forging your signature, etc.) property, inheritance, falsifying information for gain or forcing you to do it
- ☐ refusing to support children, manipulating divorce process
- ☐ withholding funds for basic needs

EMOTIONAL

- ☐ yelling
- ☐ screaming
- ☐ put-downs
- ☐ name-calling
- ☐ profanity
- ☐ mind rape
- ☐ emotional incest

PHYSICAL

- ☐ hitting
- ☐ slapping
- ☐ pushing
- ☐ spanking to the point of physical bruising or wounds

SEXUAL

- ☐ touching or penetrating the genital area
- ☐ teasing about body
- ☐ sexual humor
- ☐ sexual misinformation
- ☐ exposure to pornography

SPIRITUAL

- ☐ punitive and angry messages about God
- ☐ self-righteousness
- ☐ negative messages about sex
- ☐ modeling unhealthy lifestyle
- ☐ shame-based religion

Emotional Abuse

Most of us are familiar with the common symptoms of emotional abuse, such as yelling, screaming, put-downs, name-calling, and profanity. But most have not heard the concepts of mind rape and emotional incest.

Consider the case of Vivian, whose parent constantly referred to her as "a big dummy" every time she made a mistake. The continual tearing down of Vivian's confidence resulted in an adult who questioned her intelligence and good judgment.

We are conditioned through adult authority to think and act in ways that are considered acceptable. That is fine unless the conditioning is degrading, suppressive, manipulative, or abusive.

Mind Rape

Menticide, the word coined by psychiatrist and holocaust survivor Dr. Joost A.M. Meerloo[5] , is defined as the systematic and intentional undermining of a person's conscious mind. It's the robbing of one's independent opinions. Dr. Meerloo published the book *The Rape of the Mind: The Psychology of Thought Control*,[6] which covers the aspects of brainwashing. The term "rape of the mind" is

5 https://www.google.com/url?q=https://www.nytimes.com/1976/11/26/archives/dr-joost-meerloo-is-dead-at-73-was-authority-on-brainwashing.html&sa=D&source=editors&ust=1632420162049000&usg=AOvVaw-14R2UjlSlKqzjV0QoZAm6z

6 *The Rape of the Mind: The Psychology of Thought Control, Menticide, and Brainwashing* Meerloo, Joost A. M., Hauraki Publishing, 2015.

not just used in the trauma therapy world today, but it also defines what happens to prisoners of war and civilians in communist-run countries.

Dr. Meerloo predicted that through the use of mass media, modern technology would be one of the most powerful ways to brainwash people without using prison confinement and without their consent or awareness. Keep in mind that in the 1950s, the only form of media was radio and television. Even when it had the potential for so much good, he saw the threat it presented. And it does present a danger.

Media is very influential in shaping our thoughts and is most dangerous when we allow it to "think" for us and entertain the impressionable minds of children for hours.

How about you—did you grow up with a parent or caregiver who did not allow you any expression of an opinion that in any way threatened their expectations? Maybe it wasn't a parent or caregiver; perhaps it was someone you admire, a romantic partner, or an authority figure you wanted to impress.

Emotional abuse can go hand in hand with sexual or physical abuse. The abuse occurs, and with it comes the instruction on what thoughts to think concerning the abuse and how to feel about it. Very manipulative actions are in play when this happens. We have to not only heal from those things but make sure we don't unconsciously mimic them by manipulating others.

Emotional Incest

Emotional incest[7] is an unhealthy parent-child dynamic. The parent looks to the child for emotional support and connection instead of looking to another adult for such help. This unhealthy relationship can occur when an adult (the parent) loses their spouse (through death, divorce, separation), single motherhood, or a parent who is not getting the proper emotional support from their spouse. Though it's unintentional, the long-term effects reach far and have sticky tentacles.

When a child becomes a "partner" to the parent, it produces an unhealthy balance of power. The child is too emotionally immature to handle an adult's level of responsibility, resulting in a love-hate relationship.

These children grow to be adults who have difficulty setting boundaries or meeting their own needs, whether the relationship is personal or work-related. They may have self-esteem issues, abuse drugs and alcohol or have compulsions that revolve around work, sex, home environment, or food.

As a young child, Rob was the emotional support for his mother, who was married to Rob's dad, an emotionally unavailable man. Rob's dad was the life of any party, very personable and available to everyone except his family. His dad was self-absorbed and oblivious to the needs of his family.

---

7 https://www.goodtherapy.org/blog/emotional-covert-incest-when-parents-make-their-kids-partners-0914165

Rob entered therapy after struggling in his marriage. He was obsessive over his home, schedule, work, and successes. Rob struggled with people pleasing because he always accommodated his mother's needs, which transferred into an adult with a type-A personality. He was the workaholic with the packed schedule, looking to accommodate yet making sure everyone did everything to his standard. He was used to being leaned on but was unable to maintain the weight of everyone's dependence. The dependence that he fostered even though he resented that everyone was so "needy."

Always in overdrive, his need to control the outcome of everything was driving a wedge between him and his wife. His wife was defensive, feeling like she could never do anything right, and felt pushed to the side because he had other commitments, was overworked, or put things and other people before her.

Sound familiar? Take some time to journal some of your thoughts.

Physical Abuse

Over the last twenty to thirty years, a significant amount of focus has been on physical abuse. Today it is generally accepted that it is never appropriate to harm a child physically. Sadly, in earlier generations, it was common practice to whip children into obedience. A violent environment where someone breaks or throws things in rage or harms animals also damages a child.

If you were physically disciplined in a way that left marks, you were the victim of physical abuse. It is never justified to hit children with either a hand or object in a manner that leaves streaks, cuts, or bruises.

Financial Abuse

Financial Abuse[8] is defined as the behavior of controlling a person's ability to gain, use, and maintain money. Financial abuse is often found in elderly abuse cases, domestic violence cases, and divorce and custody cases, to name a few. According to the National Network to End Domestic Violence (NNEDV), *"financial abuse is one of the most powerful methods of keeping a survivor trapped in an abusive relationship and deeply diminishes the victim's ability to stay safe after leaving an abusive partner."*

8 https://nnedv.org/wp-content/uploads/2019/07/Library_EJ_Financial_Abuse_Fact_Sheet.pdf

Research[9] shows that financial abuse occurs in 99 percent of domestic violence cases. The NNEDV put out a list[10] of behaviors associated with financially abusive people. They are:

- Forbidding the person to work.
- Sabotaging work or employment opportunities by stalking or harassing the person at the workplace or causing the person to lose her/his job by physically battering prior to important meetings or interviews.
- Forbidding the person from attending job training or advancement opportunities.
- Controlling how all of the money is spent.
- Not including the person in investment or banking decisions.
- Not allowing the person access to bank accounts.
- Withholding money or giving "an allowance."
- Forcing the person to write bad checks or file fraudulent tax returns.
- Running up large amounts of debt on joint accounts.
- Refusing to work or contribute to the family income.
- Withholding funds for the person or children to obtain basic needs such as food and medicine.
- Hiding assets.

---

9 https://centerforfinancialsecurity.files.wordpress.com/2015/04/adams2011.pdf

10 https://nnedv.org/content/about-financial-abuse/

- Stealing the person's identity, property, or inheritance.
- Forcing the person to work in a family business without pay.
- Refusing to pay bills and ruining the person's credit score.
- Forcing the person to turn over public benefits or threatening to turn the victim in for "cheating or misusing benefits."
- Filing false insurance claims.
- Refusing to pay or evading child support or manipulating the divorce process by drawing it out by hiding or not disclosing assets.

Sexual Abuse

Child Sexual Abuse

What are the latest statistics on child sexual abuse? As of this writing, the statistics vary greatly, but the estimate is one out of three girls and one out of six boys have experienced some type of sexual abuse by the time they are eighteen years old.

However, the actual number reported is not the same. According to the most recent reported statistics, one out of ten children is sexually abused before age eighteen, and 60 percent of child sexual abuse victims never tell anyone.

Often women have a flawed concept of what it means to have been sexually abused. Sexual abuse involves many more categories than intercourse. Intercourse is only one form.

A simple definition of sexual abuse is when a child of any age (including adolescents, who some falsely believe are old enough to "know better") is sexually exploited by an adult for that adult's own purpose or gratification. So, inappropriate touching or kissing, therefore, also constitutes sexual abuse.

There are two kinds of sexual violations:

1. Overt — This involves specific physical contact. Overt abuse includes fondling breasts or genitals, masturbation of the child or adult, sexual kinds of kissing, oral sex performed on either the adult or child, or penetration with the hand, penis, or an object.
2. Covert — This involves abuse that occurs without direct physical contact. Examples include inappropriate nudity, forcing a child to watch others being sexual, exposing a child to pornography, or spying on a child bathing or dressing. Sexual teasing, inappropriate comments about body development, or sexual activity, is also abusive.

Another confusing misconception about sexual abuse is how the child's body often responds to the sexual abuse occurring. Our bodies are designed to respond and, physically speaking, the body doesn't discern unhealthy touch from healthy touch.

Only our mindsets can determine unhealthy touch, and as a child, we were probably not taught this. Consequently, we don't realize we have been abused. In addition, there is no maturity to understand that just because our bodies responded does not mean we consented or that the action was appropriate.

Adult Sexual Assault and Intimate Partner Sexual Violence

Every sixty-eight seconds, an American is sexually assaulted, and every nine minutes, that American is a child. So that's roughly 1,271 sexual assaults, 160 of them committed against children, in twenty-four hours. Meanwhile, only 2.5 percent of all perpetrators, that's twenty-five out of every 1,000, end up in prison.

According to RAINN (Rape, Abuse, Incest National Network):[11]

> *"there are many different terms to refer to sexual violence that occurs within intimate partnerships, including: intimate partner sexual violence, domestic violence, intimate partner rape, marital rape, and spousal rape. No matter what term is used or how the relationship is defined, it is never okay to engage in sexual activity without someone's consent."*

Whether the violence is by a partner, acquaintance, or stranger, it is never the fault of the person who was

11 https://www.rainn.org/articles/intimate-partner-sexual-violence

harmed. Never. To believe so means that we believe we are in control of someone else's actions. This is never the case. Every person is responsible for their own actions and reactions. It's a faulty belief system that has us taking responsibility for the actions of others.

I know firsthand about feeling responsible for someone else's actions. The year was 2001 and I was a college sophomore. I was living on my own and partying my way through that college life. After all, I was at LSU (Louisiana State University) and keeping up with that famous LSU social life. And believe me—I had my fair share of fun!

One night, after partying late at a local bar, I got a ride home from an acquaintance. He was a friend of a friend. I didn't personally know this guy. He attended an out-of-state SEC university. It wasn't unusual for out-of-town college students to come to Baton Rouge for the weekend and party with LSU students. So, running into him was a bit of a surprise, but also it wasn't.

Supposedly, he had other friends in Baton Rouge and was just down visiting. He dropped me off at my apartment, and at the time, my roommate was not home. Within minutes he was in my bedroom, and he was not leaving.

What happened next, I never spoke of to anyone. I buried it. Until I started writing this book, that is.

I buried it so deeply in my mind that it was no longer a conscious memory. I had trauma blocked it to the place that years later, twenty to be exact, I couldn't even recall details of what happened, the guy's name, or the exact time frame it occurred.

I was sexually assaulted and somehow felt it was my fault. And if something was my fault, then it was my responsibility to own it and move forward by doing better. I owned it by telling no one about "my mistake." What faulty thinking after something so traumatic, right?

What I did in the years to follow was avoid. I gave up my apartment, withdrew from LSU, and moved to another state. I thought leaving LSU and enrolling at a different university would make me better. I thought moving out of state would make me better. I thought breaking up with a college boyfriend would make me better. I thought staying silent about my low self-esteem and self-hatred would make me better. I thought partying more and engaging in riskier behaviors would somehow give me back the self-worth I had lost, because after all, I was in control. Or so I thought.

What was in control was a faulty belief system coupled with a lack of tools needed to dig up what was "no longer affecting me."

Spiritual Abuse

Spiritual Abuse involves being "hit over the head" with the Bible or religious tradition and doctrine. It means being motivated into right action by shame and fear of damnation instead of promoting a desire for a right relationship with God. It's receiving angry and punitive messages about God instead of a portrayal of a loving Father who desires the best for those who follow him.

If you were physically, emotionally, or sexually abused by someone who represented spiritual authority in your life, you automatically are a victim of spiritual abuse.

Because of our limited human capacity to understand spiritual things, we often base our view of God mainly on the early spiritual figures in our life. Think, then, about the impact of experiencing abuse at the hands of one who represents God—this has the potential to create years of unhealthy, unhelpful, and unproductive living.

If you haven't already—take some time to read through the types of abuse on the left-hand side of the page and see what resonates with you. The things that happened to you were not okay and will never be acceptable. But you are okay, and you are acceptable. We are, according to Ephesians 1:6, *"accepted into the beloved."*

Let's pause. That was heavy. I want you to take some time to debrief. Maybe you need to talk to a friend right now or your significant other. You have possibly had some real eye-opening moments, and it's important to take care of yourself. Spending time in prayer and reading the word of God is vital to renewing your heart and mind after doing such a deep dive into your past.

Maybe you are thinking, "Vera, I have been in therapy for years, and believe me, I have already identified where my traumas are!" No matter where you are currently, take some time to process this.

Phase Three
The Aftermath

"We may not control the storm,
but what comes after is ours to create."
— Vera

Effects of Abandonment and Abuse

Our brain stems, which are responsible for our fight-or-flight reactions, are fully developed at birth. However, our temporal lobes, which receive input from our senses, are responsible for emotional development over time and by exposure to life experiences. Do you see what that means?

If our early life experiences are healthy and we receive proper nurture and care, we develop healthy emotional coping and appropriate fight-or-flight responses.

Our brains are like huge filing cabinets. Under normal circumstances, we experience something, deal with it mentally and emotionally, and "file" it in that cabinet. However, the trauma that never gets filed away due to its ongoing nature or lack of "filing" tools has nowhere to go.

Though our brain stems regulate our flight-or-fight, they don't distinguish between past and present. So that unresolved trauma is left hanging out there and resurfaces when triggered. And because the brain stem can't tell the difference between past and present, unresolved traumatic experiences continue to surface, creating havoc in that person's life.

However, even the most balanced individual with the most solid emotional foundation can experience something so traumatic that their responses get out of whack.

Such is the case with my client Olivia. When Olivia was a young girl, her mother had a physical medical issue that resulted in a permanent cognitive impairment. Olivia was left emotionally abandoned by her mother as her mother mentally decompensated.

Though close to her father, due to his need to work to support the family and tend to a wife who was not mentally competent, he was unable to provide the support Olivia needed. As her mother's life spiraled out of control, so did Olivia's. Within a couple of months of her mother's breakdown, Olivia was smoking marijuana and drinking alcohol. She was not yet a teenager. She shared:

> *"My life turned. I became "different" from what my friend knew, and now the only people that accepted me were the ones doing drugs and walking the wild life. I was looking for an outlet, and my new friends gave me one. My dad couldn't keep up with my mom and me, and I guess my mom needed him more. I had no one to explain this to me and no way to handle it."*

It took years of toxic responses and bad choices before Olivia found her way out. But she did get out. You can get out too.

Whether the tragedy was a week ago or a childhood ago, identifying your reactions and tracing them back will help you face them and "file" them.

Paraphrased from the book *The Betrayal Bond* by Patrick Carnes,[12] the following "reactions" information is helpful information. This book is an excellent tool for trauma survivors who struggle in relationships or not knowing how to get out of a toxic relationship.

Reactions

Sometimes to make sense of a traumatic experience, you take on the blame yourself. Survivors' guilt is an example. These reactions are us "taking the blame, shame, and guilt" for what has happened.

Toxic Bonding

Due to a hurt inner child, this psychological response to abuse or abandonment (can be any of the violations or abandonment mentioned in previous phases) causes the abused person to form an unhealthy bond with the person who hurt them.

Not everyone who experiences abuse or abandonment develops a trauma bond. But for those who do, the process begins when the victim feels sorry for the abuser. Then, although the abuser has hurt them significantly, they still attempt to help them.

They give trust, although the abuser has proven to be untrustworthy time and time again. They attempt to be understood by the very person hurting them, but in

12 *The Betrayal Bond: Breaking Free of Exploitive Relationships* Carnes, Patrick J., Health Communications, Inc., 1997, 2019.

reality, that person doesn't care enough to understand the thoughts and emotions of anyone but themselves.

The abuser only feeds himself and manipulates the abused into believing they desire them and care about them. An extreme example is Stockholm Syndrome, a condition in which hostages, during captivity, develop a psychological bond with their captors.

Blame, Shame, and Guilt

Sometimes to make sense of a traumatic experience, the victimized ones take on the blame themselves. They carry shame because they feel they were willing participants of the trauma. Sometimes, they carry guilt because they got free when others did not. Shame plays a significant role here as well because the survivor has a sense of unworthiness for surviving.

Examples of survivor's guilt include soldiers or other first responders who survive an attack or other hostile, life-threatening situations, surviving a car accident that killed others, or surviving a life-threatening illness like cancer when others haven't. In my personal story of sexual assault, thought it wasn't mine to assume, for years I absolutely took on the blame and carried the shame and guilt. I got free of it. So can you.

Blocking

Trauma blocking happens when a person successfully blocks out traumatic thoughts, engages in unhealthy behaviors that block, numbs, or distract them. Examples can include everything from excessive working, staying busy, engaging in hobbies, excessive TV or social media, binge drinking, drug use, and compulsive shopping, eating, or exercise.

It's important to note that most trauma blocking behaviors give significant relief and feel good but never last and must be repeated, sometimes in ever-increasing toxic measures to the detriment of the traumatized person.

Repetition

Repetition is the repeating of behaviors that mimic early childhood traumatic experiences. Many people who are abusers were once victims themselves. They are copying their abuser's actions.

The repetition can also be a subconscious effort to find someone to rescue them from their pain and make their lives better. Sadly, this often doesn't work out well and leaves the survivor seeking toxic or emotionally unhealthy people, which results in trauma repetitions.

Dissociation

Dissociation[13] happens when there is an emotional or physical disconnection between a person's reality and their memories, feelings, behaviors, perceptions, or sense of self. Those diagnosed with PTSD often experience dissociation and describe it as an "out of body" experience.

We experience a small form of dissociation when we daydream. This is normal. But someone with long-term, persistent dissociative episodes feels like they live in one daydream after the next.

Various psychiatric conditions can have the symptom of dissociation, not just dissociative disorders. Anxiety, depression, borderline personality disorder, epilepsy, OCD, PTSD, and schizophrenia can all have an element of dissociation.

Hypervigilance

A heightened state of alertness marks hypervigilance. They are very aware of their surroundings to the extreme, like living in a war zone when there has not been any threat of war for years. The tones of other people's voices may affect them significantly. They have a fear of others judging them, and any sense of uncertainty is intolerable.

Those with hypervigilance feel as if they live in a constant state of anxiety and often have impulsive behaviors due to the possible threat of their fear becoming

13 *American Psychiatric Association Diagnostic and Statistical Manual of Mental Disorders*, DSM 5th Ed., 2013

a reality. They live in that state where they are "waiting for the bottom to fall out."

The hypervigilant, "always on guard" mindset has an unfounded source of fear. There is no valid threat. This inability to identify a threat should tell them that their reaction to the possibility of something bad happening, going wrong, or not working out is disproportionate to the reality. Constantly going through memories or scripting out future events in their heads to always be on alert and ready for a negative experience just in case it happens should not be their focus.

Strugglers with hypervigilance are more likely to be sensitive to physical pain, stress, anxiety, anger, grief, loss, avoidance, or socially challenging situations and relationships that involve becoming emotionally close or involve any type of confrontation.

Consequently, it's helpful to monitor our thinking and evaluate our thoughts for credibility. Vague, uneasy feelings having no apparent cause are then addressed with the faith of a heart entrusted to God. Make sense?

Loss of Faith and Trust

Deep fear of trusting others and a loss of faith in humanity, our religious beliefs, or even ourselves sometimes happens when we experience trauma from an unexpected source.

After a traumatic experience, we can view the world and the people around us as dangerous. Many survivors of complex traumas walk away from their religious beliefs or upbringings, doubting their ability to have good judgment.

Over the years counseling survivors of sexual abuse at the hands of a priest or pastor or someone in a religious role, I've come to understand that this enters into another category other than just sexual abuse. It is spiritual abuse as well.

For the abused, it left a confusing message about God. Questions like, "How can a loving God allow suffering and abuse to happen?" surface. For the survivor, it is the ultimate betrayal.

Physical Pain

Body hypervigilance is often the result of abuse, abandonment, and high levels of stress. The body, not just the mind, is chronically tense, bracing for potential impact (trauma).Chronic stress causes the stress hormone, cortisol, to be released. Continual release of cortisol produces inflammation. Inflammation produces pain. The higher the level of inflammation, the higher the pain level.

Unhealthy Pleasure

According to Carnes, in his book *The Betrayal Bond*,[14] trauma pleasure is *"seeking or finding pleasure and stimulation in the presence of extreme danger, violence, risk, or shame."* The high thrill and risky behaviors identify this reaction subset and continuing to seek higher levels of risk is the norm here. Thus, gambling and risky life choices are habitual even though the results are destroying them and those around them.

They don't do well with downtime or solitude and are more prone to abusing drugs like cocaine and speed-like other medicines. They may engage in high-risk or violent sexual activity and often associate with toxic or unhealthy people.

Abstinence

Compulsive deprivation, abstinence, is found in moments of success, high stress, shame, or anxiety.

I've had therapy clients who engage in patterns of compulsive saving (saving to the point of going without basic needs), poverty obsessions (fear of not having enough), success avoidance (limiting themselves in personal and professional growth), self-neglect, underachieving, and workaholism.

This compulsive abstinence causes them to go long periods with little to no food, sometimes developing into

14 The Betrayal Bond: Breaking Free of Exploitive Relationships Carnes, Patrick J., Health Communications, Inc., 1997, 2019.

eating disorders. Or they deny themselves basic medical care, new shoes, clothing, or living and housing necessities. They often hoard money and feel guilty for spending it on legitimate needs.

The compulsive deprivers have a hard time with free time and rarely engage in fun things or play. They skip vacations because of lack of time or money—the lack of time or money is a distorted perception not based on facts. The reality is they don't see themselves as having enough personal value to deserve a vacation.

Phase Four

Relationship Attachments

"The propensity to make strong emotional bonds to particular individuals [is] a basic component of human nature."
—John Bowlby

The deprivations caused by emotional, physical, sexual, spiritual, and financial abandonment and abuse relate to an important psychological phenomenon known as "attachment theory".[15]

Attachment theory states our earliest relationships with our childhood caregivers set the stage for how we, in turn, build relationships in our adult life.

The psychiatrist and psychoanalyst John Bowlby first began examining attachment by observing the connection between infants and mothers from the earliest moments of life through early childhood development. Bowlby suggested that *"children come into the world biologically pre-programmed to form attachments with others because this will help them to survive."*[16]

Let's think about that for a moment. We were created for relationships—it's necessary for our survival. Wow! The details of our Creator, huh?

There are four types of attachment styles. Three of the four are insecure attachment styles, and one is a secure attachment. The ability to have and maintain secure

15 https://www.naadac.org/assets/2416/michael_bricker_adultattachment_ac16_ho.pdf

16 https://www.simplypsychology.org/bowlby.html#:~:text=Bowlby's%20evolutionary%20theory%20of%20attachment,This%20is%20called%20monotropy

attachments begins with healthy childhood physical and emotional development. Secure parents raise secure children.

What a Secure Parent Looks Like

They are consistent in their availability to the needs of their child and parent with warm responses. Secure parents attend to their child's feelings and don't just provide a roof over the child's head and clothes on their back but provide emotional support too. They show up and show out!

They put their phones down and pay attention to what is going on in their child's world—emotionally, physically, socially, and spiritually. When secure attachments don't happen in childhood development, it leaves a child in a state of chronic stress, anxiety, and fear—it can stunt their development and prevent them from reaching specific important social, emotional, and spiritual milestones. The lack of secure parenting is what leads to the development of insecure attachment styles.

Let's look at the three types of insecure attachments for your information and self-evaluation. The fourth attachment style, secure, is the goal you are working toward (in all relationships) and is part of Chapter Two. Are you ready? Here we go.

ANXIOUS ATTACHMENT

- ☐ Low self-esteem
- ☐ A struggle with self-worth in relationships
- ☐ Sensitivity if rejected by a partner or loved one
- ☐ Feelings of being unworthy of love
- ☐ The ongoing need for reassurance that you are loved, worthy, or good enough
- ☐ Fear of abandonment

Three types of insecure attachment styles:[17]

The commonality between all three insecure attachment styles is difficulty forming and maintaining stable and healthy relationships with others. Sit with that for a minute but don't let it intimidate you. This is not a book of judgment. Instead, it's a manual for healing, specifically yours.

Anxious Attachment Style (also referred to as anxious-preoccupied attachment style or anxious-ambivalent attachment style)

Excessive worry about other people's perceptions of us and a strong desire for extreme closeness in relationships mark anxious attachment.

Look at the anxious attachment style box to the left. Do you see yourself? Check off what is relatable and add your own if it's not there.

Anxious attachment adults desire complete emotional connection to others but find others reluctant to get as close as they would want them to. They describe themselves as being fine without close relationships (best friend, significant other, etc.) but worry that others don't appreciate and value them as much as they value others. You see the internal conflict here?

17 https://www.choosingtherapy.com/abandonment-issues/ http://labs.psychology.illinois.edu/~rcfraley/attachment.htm

While they can think highly of others, they struggle with low self-esteem personally. In relationships, they need approval as much as they don't like to admit it. They need their partner or friend to be responsive, and if they don't get that, their minds drift into a place of worrisome speculation. They crave a high level of intimacy, so much so that they can appear to others as overly dependent on their significant other, family members, or friends.

When in adult relationships, they can experience suspiciousness and intense jealousy of others (especially if their partner gives someone else time or attention—even if it was healthy or respectful). When in an unhealthy mindset, they can become clingy, appear desperate, and be preoccupied with their relationship.

They may not have other close friends (best friends) or other people in their lives with whom they can be vulnerable because they rely on that from their partner and only their partner. And the tiniest bit of disappointment from the partner can be hurtful to their already low self-esteem.

At times, having their partner in their presence is their perceived solution to getting rid of their anxious and emotional neediness brought on by suspicious thoughts and fears of being alone. It's the equivalent of covering a gushing wound with an adhesive bandage. If you manage to stop the blood flow, it won't be long before the wound seeps again.

Anxious attachment styles affect us in our workplace, as can the other two insecure attachment styles. Intimate, sexual relationships are affected as well.

In intimacy, sex is sometimes used for approval. As a result, the person falls in love quickly but may, at times, also mistrust their partner.

When anxiously attached people view things negatively, have unrealistic expectations, paranoia, and intermittent distrust of their partner combined with worry about personal self-worth and attractiveness, the result is lousy sex.

The thing is, it's not the sex that's bad. Instead, the unhelpful mindset of the anxiously attached person results in the inability to experience satisfying and mutually pleasurable sex.

An anxious attachment personality is usually rooted in inconsistent, inattentive, or unresponsive parenting in their childhood. However, keep in mind that this unavailable parenting is not always conscious.

One of my friends shared with me her husband's experience growing up with a mentally ill mother. Veronica said:

> *"He rarely speaks of his mom's mental illness. Really, he's probably only ever talked about it at length twice in the forty-plus years we are married. He told me about how she would sit and seemed not to know he was there. Sometimes she would do things for them* [her children], *like sew a button on a shirt or something. And, sometimes, he would call her name and call her name, and she would never answer.*
>
> *Of course, he was little and didn't really understand what was wrong. He just accepted it. It didn't make him*

> *needy. It made him very self-reliant. Almost too much, ya' know?"*

A parent or caregiver may be attentive, supportive, and appear to have it together. And at other times, they are disconnected and unable to attend to the child's needs. When a parent is sometimes available and sometimes totally unresponsive, a child learns at a young age, "I can't count on you when I need you."

The advent of smart devices and the "internet at our fingertips" has resulted in today's parents and partners in relationships engaging in inconsistent and inattentive parenting without awareness of it.

One of the number one reasons for this inconsistency is the SMARTPHONE! The virtual connection gets more time and attention than is given to making an actual connection with the child. A curated link that gives the appearance of community and relationship can never take the place of a real connection and relationship. The sociability purported via social media is contrived and has little value in promoting healthy relationships.

Sound advice on this is to stop posting *about* your children on social media and give attention *to* them. Converse with them. Have the hard conversations. Engage in activities that interest and develop your child. Activities that don't involve games on a smartphone or a game box.

Inconsistency sends mixed messages to a child while growing up. The child can't figure out how to read the parents' behaviors and what to expect in the future. So naturally, that creates a lot of unknowns for a child and produces anxiety.

Emotional Hunger

There is a concept in the attachment theory world called "emotional hunger," where the parent or caregiver seeks emotional or physical connection and closeness with the child to simply satisfy their own needs and not that of the child's. These parents can seem overprotective, strict, controlling at times, and intrusive with a bombarding of questions.

They can attempt to present themselves in perfect light or that they are not the problem. The adult may do this unknowingly or not fully aware because it has become an automatic response. After all, that's how they were parented too.

Do you see how this continues behavior patterns over generations and not necessarily just "the way they are" (genetics)? So it's no surprise that an anxious attachment style in a caregiver can condition an anxious attachment style in a child.

Avoidant Attachment Style (also referred to as anxious-avoidant attachment style or avoidant-dismissive attachment style)

Did you check any of the following emotional wounds of childhood abandonment like not being heard, not receiving emotional care, empathy, or nurturing, or no expression of affection? If so, you might want to pay a little closer attention to this attachment type.

This style is challenging because these adults appear to be independent, confident, and self-sufficient on the surface. And they are, but it comes with a bit of a darker side.

Though the anxious attachment style is pretty easy to spot, the avoidant attachment style requires a closer look.

Avoidant attachment people feel they are okay without close emotional relationships—they don't feel it's necessary for survival. They prefer not to depend on others or have others depend on them too much.

These people often are fun to be around and have many friends, but once a relationship turns toward vulnerability and closeness, they shut the connection down. If they don't shut the relationship down, they may, instead, work hard to keep the relationship fun, light, and peaceful, all the while keeping all complex emotions away.

Avoidant attachment adults can be defensive and struggle to build long-lasting, deep relationships. They don't struggle to make friends and are very enjoyable to be around—it's only when a relationship becomes vulnerable that they move on to something less threatening. So, if you're not looking for a vulnerable and deep connection to someone, then avoidant attachment style people will love you!

In their childhood, their parents or caregivers were more than likely emotionally unavailable. Please note I said emotionally unavailable—that doesn't mean physically inaccessible. You may have grown up in a home with physically present but emotionally disconnected parents. In some cases, the parents may not have tolerated the child displaying any emotions the parents perceived as negative or inappropriate.

If a situation arose in which the parent felt a possible negative emotion or outburst was looming, the parent then engaged in behaviors to immediately shut that down, persuade the child to feel a different way and display a more acceptable emotion, or attempt to distract or change the topic of conversation.

Caregivers can, sometimes unconsciously, take it a step further and become more and more distant as the emotional tension between the child and caregiver grows. When the child does something to gain emotional closeness or attention from the parent, the parent in return doesn't respond or becomes distant and avoidant.

These types of parents may tell their children things like, "toughen up," "it's not that big of a deal," "you are being dramatic," or even worse, "don't even start with those emotions—no one cares to see the tears!" These parents often have unrealistic expectations for their children to be independent and well-behaved, yet they don't provide the emotional and social support to model these skills.

Children with emotionally unavailable parents become adults who believe that they can't rely on people. You see, their parents reinforced this belief when they didn't show up for their kids emotionally.

Disorganized Attachment Style (also referred to as fearful-avoidant attachment style)

The Disorganized Attachment style is not a combination of the previous two mentioned above. The previously mentioned styles are the organized ones. The avoidant attachments are consistent with avoiding hard emotions, and anxious attachments are consistent with anxious and worrisome thoughts. But the disorganized attachment style is just that—quite disorganized!

In other words, it's the most complex insecure attachment style of the three and most often found in people who have been physically, emotionally (verbally), or sexually abused in childhood.

For these types, their childhood consisted of some kind of marked fear. For example, childhoods marked by unpredictable and inconsistent caregiving result in children who experience feeling insecure and unsafe. That is where the fear was born.

To illustrate, when the child personally experienced abuse by the caregiver or witnessed the caregiver abusing someone else, this reinforced the fearful thoughts and solidified the belief that security and safety didn't exist.

The child grows up not trusting the caregiver—which is a natural response and not wrong due to what they have endured and seen. The child can go back and forth trying to seek closeness from the caregiver but can also reject the caregiver's proximity due to fear.

A primary characteristic of this attachment style is the mixed feelings the person has about close relationships.

They desire to be emotionally close in relationships, but on the other hand, feel uncomfortable with it.

If they are in a romantic relationship, they often feel unworthy and suspicious of their partner. In general, they struggle with trusting others (their partner, family members, friends, coworkers, bosses, religious leaders, acquaintances, etc.).

Another characteristic of the disorganized attachment style is how inconsistent these people can be. They have developed these inconsistencies in their adult life due to a very disorganized and inconsistent childhood. As a result, they struggle to process and cope with anything complicated life throws at them as adults.

Experiencing any adversity is difficult for them. They may shut down and have the inability to cope in a healthy manner. This attachment style is often a high risk for various mental health problems—depression, borderline personality disorder, substance abuse, or all of these.

Disorganized attachment adults desire relationships (which is one of the differences from the avoidant attachment styles). Yet, they don't want to let anyone in (fear) because they feel people closest to them will hurt and betray them. As adults, they are waiting for the rejection, betrayal, and abandonment to happen—as if it's just a matter of time.

This attachment style lends itself to the self-fulfilling prophecy concept. Those struggling with disorganized attachment often find themselves in relationships that induce fear, which confirms their theory of not trusting other people. As a result, they repeat or allow traumatic, unhealthy relationships in their lives and may struggle to form healthy relationships with their kids.

It is important to remember that having one of these three insecure attachment styles does not mean having a mental disorder or disease. Yes, insecure attachment styles can cause distress in relationships, but that's why you are reading this book.

I'll help you with working toward a healthy mindset of secure attachments. Then, in Chapter Two of this book, I explain further how to overcome insecure attachments and develop healthy, secure attachments with others.

After reading and thinking through the abandonment types, which, if any, have you experienced? Circle the ones that apply to you. Which do you identify with the most?

Phase Five

Avoidance

"Avoiding problems you need to face is avoiding the life you need to live."
— Paulo Coelho

It's the spring of 2021, and I am an emotional mess. The year before was a crisis year, and I was already exhausted from counseling so many through pandemic-induced situations for which they had no prior point of reference.

I was in an ongoing health battle with MRSA. I was physically in a great deal of pain and compounding this was my body's resistance to nearly every antibiotic treatment available. I had been hospitalized two years before with a MRSA infection that required surgical removal. Not wanting to go back to the hospital was weighing heavy and taking a toll not just physically but also mentally. Additionally, I was now entering into territory demanding skills that made me feel like a bit of an imposter.

I was writing this book, which my business coach, Alli, says is like punching yourself in the nose every day. Alli's not wrong about that. Since I have a "superwoman" trait, I consistently work to keep a balanced life and schedule. But by this point, I was seriously off track and had no idea the necessary trek through my past would unravel me. *duh*

I had clients willing to share parts of their stories for my book, so I interviewed them and asked a mentor and confidant to interview me. My interviews—wow! Several hours long, those sessions had me revealing things I had never previously disclosed, and they wrecked me.

No wonder a few weeks later, I found myself nervously sitting in this small room. The taupe-colored walls, meant to be soothing, were not helping in any way to quiet the thoughts floating around in my head. Directly across from me sat the therapist. Her name was Nigerian and unfamiliar to me, so instead of focusing on what had brought me to her office, I focused on the fact that I didn't know how to pronounce her name correctly. I mean, why focus on my serious issues when I can avoid them by focusing on the therapist with the exotic accent and challenging name pronunciation. If you are born in Louisiana, you don't even bat an eye at unusual names, so this was a worthy challenge. And a convenient distraction.

I wasn't prepared for this and didn't know it. I've done many hard things in my life, but this was proving one of the hardest. This therapist got herself a therapist.

What prompted the therapy appointment? The week before, I found myself in the middle of the absolute worst panic attack of my life. So bad was the episode that I thought it was good to start calling psychiatric hospitals for self-admitting during some part of it.

You can laugh at this point. It feels irrational even to say out loud, but the thoughts, feelings, and physical pain all mixed were just too much to bear at that moment.

I can't count how many people I have helped walk through panic and moments like I was experiencing, but I just couldn't seem to do it for myself. I felt like a failure, unable to help myself when I had helped so many.

I was in a cycle of chaos. A spin cycle. The miserable hamster wheel was rolling along, active but going nowhere. Whatever one calls that total, unending, no way out cyclone of mental and emotional angst, there I was. Those moments you don't forget—I mean, how can you?

Jesus, RESCUE ME! Do You hear me, God? Yeah, it's Vera! I need a lifeline here!

It was one of those I-feel-like-I'm-dying experiences. After the therapist had listened to me talk for nearly an hour straight, she said, "Vera, I want you to think about this question and have an answer for me the next time I see you."

Yes, a question! Let's get this done. Resolution is why I'm here. I leaned in, eager for the question, ready for the work. *This is why I came. Bring on the next task. I am always prepared! Because I stay busy, busy, busy.* But was I ready for this one? I thought so.

"How do you find rest?" she asked.
"How do I find rest?" I blankly mimicked.

I paused, probably the first mental pause in the entire hour. That previous eagerness, now a pile of dread, sat in my stomach like dead weight. I felt the bubbling of hysterical laughter. And the potential for uncontrollable crying.

I was wondering if I ever really helped anyone with anything. I can't even answer this one question. As she continued talking and explaining some things, the question just kept playing over and over in my head—a sad song, stuck on repeat.

Ever the busy, busy woman, I studiously saved the question in my iPhone notes and soon headed out of her office. On my one-hour drive back home, my mind began to race with thoughts. And questions.

"Vera... What is rest to you?"
"What does that look like?"
"What day is Sabbath for you?"
"Wait, do I even have a Sabbath day?"
"Oh, my goodness—I don't know!"

Every single thought I'd had about rest involved doing something. Hitting me in the mental face like a sucker punch was the realization that I was almost always obsessively doing something. I always had a project or an event. At the same time was the revelation that I didn't know what defined rest for me.

I was fresh out of ideas. The woman that fixes everything for everyone couldn't fix herself. I needed God's mindset, not my own!

I was in a chaotic cycle, and avoidance had taken me there.

What is avoidance?

In preparing for this phase of the book, I took to the world of Facebook and asked my friends what things they were avoiding. My questions—"What things have you avoided like a bad plague? What was your reason for such avoidance?"

The responses were insightful but also confirmed my theory that not enough of us are talking about this. We are avoiding having conversations about avoiding.

I love what one friend responded: "I'm the queen of avoidance. I would rather not say publicly. LOL." Another friend said: "I have issues sharing what I've avoided."

I hear ya', sistas!

Before you feel like there's no help for you, remember that Adam and Eve were the first avoiders, starting in Genesis chapter three.

> *"Then the man and his wife heard the sound of the Lord God as he was walking in the garden in the cool of the day, and they hid from the Lord God among the trees of the garden"* (Genesis 3:8 NIV).

What causes us to avoid, you may be wondering. The answer is the conscious mind.

Before I go further, let me answer the question of what our conscious mind is. The conscious mind is the part of us that is currently aware of things, situations, and surroundings. It also accesses preconscious things such as how to wash clothes. We know how to wash clothes, but we don't keep that forefront of our thoughts. However, we can retrieve that information when we need it, unless we don't know how to wash clothes. In that case, we recall who we know who can wash clothes and where to find their phone number.

I personally never washed clothes until I was in college. Before living on my own, the dirty ones just magically appeared back in my closet, clean and ready to go.

So back to avoidance. Is avoidance a result of just simple situations that we have complicated using faulty reasoning and broken logic? Or is it more? Well, that's where the unconscious mind plays a role. Things that go undealt with are removed from our conscious minds as a self-preservation tactic and usually surface when "triggered" by a similar experience, or haunt us in our dreams and can unconsciously influence our feelings and behaviors.

I identify with my Facebook friend, who refers to herself as the "queen of avoidance." I once was that girl. The desire for avoidance creeps up into my mind still to this day. It whispers lies that seem like truths. It tries to provide me comfort and counsel, but it leaves me deceived, in denial, or worse, emotionally numb. I have to fight it with a powerful spiritual sword, and sometimes it's exhausting. And it seems easier to just give in to it rather than fight for peace.

One of the main reasons I call myself the "past queen of avoidance" is I am no longer on that throne, friends! But I was that queen for many years.

I was the girl who avoided the hard conversation with her biological father for nearly thirty-three years of my life. Do you know how many people go their whole lives and never have certain hard conversations? That thought just about haunted me, yet I didn't do anything about it for so many years. Talk about being stuck! That's more than being stuck—that's called emotional paralysis.

I justified avoidance. I had my reasons, and I am sure many of you do too. One of my friends commented on my Facebook post that it had been almost eleven years since her father passed away, and all of his things, including his hospital bag, are still in storage bins untouched. They have sat there because she doesn't want to encounter the grief all over again. It feels too much to handle. Her dad's possessions are the only tangible thing she feels she has left of him. That's a powerful example of how our mind tricks us to believe that avoidance is the solution.

Avoidance is just a temporary Band-Aid but never a forever healing.

Let's get our forever healings—let's find our peace, productivity, and purpose. So, what's the next step? By now, I hope you know the answer is information first, then evaluation.

I know it's easy to identify other people who do these things when reading through this list, but this book is for you. You are writing your Chapter Two, and to do that, you must take the time to focus on YOU—not Anxious Aunt Sally, not Momma Karen, not Psycho Boss Bob—but YOU.

I had to take this same inventory—I am right here with you cheering you on and sharing my avoidance secrets with the belief that bravery is contagious.

Two Types of Avoidance

Healthy Avoidance

Healthy, positive avoidance aligns with healthy boundaries in Chapter Two, Phase Four of your book. You map out your strategy for new default behavior there.

Unhealthy Avoidance

In this phase, we learn about unhealthy avoidance and its two subtypes—unhealthy internal avoidance and unhealthy external avoidance.

Here's where you learn how to identify your avoidance patterns and take an avoidance inventory. I know that sounds about as appealing as a slide down a razor blade, but you bought this book because you are tired of being stuck.

Remember, this is a process, and this book is a guide. Many have traveled through the avoidance inventory before you and come out safe and whole. You can too. So, deep breath and continue.

Under both types of avoidance, there are subtypes. First, there is positive internal avoidance and positive external avoidance. Second, there is negative internal avoidance and negative external avoidance.

Let's take inventory by starting with an explanation and a definition.

Avoidance begins in our thoughts. In the beginning, avoidance can seem like we are succeeding in creating a positive outcome. Why? Because by its very nature, to avoid is to succeed in keeping away from a dangerous or undesirable experience.

And with certain avoidance behaviors, we do have positive results—we avoid speeding because we don't want to get a ticket!

But not all avoidance is healthy.

Stay with me, and I will show you where unhealthy avoidance leads. See if you recognize yourself. Spoiler alert, everyone recognizes themselves here because we all avoid something.

Unhealthy Internal Avoidance

- ☐ Your thought process is "I can't ask for help," so you continue in an anxious, frazzled existence. You don't internally process hard emotions such as grief, guilt, shame. You won't even let your mind go there, causing unwarranted reactions that recur in other situations.
- ☐ You lack self-awareness—people may bring up suggestions to you, give you feedback, but your mind says otherwise as if there is absolutely no way they are telling the truth about you or that the suggestion would work. (This is one that most people rarely identify in themselves. So if someone has told you this in the past, you may want to check it.)
- ☐ You lack rest in your mind. Your thoughts are unsettled—you find yourself worrying and overanalyzing just about everything, so it causes you to avoid various things listed below in the negative external avoidance box.
- ☐ You block every hard emotion, thought, or feeling out of your mind, using busyness or distractions to keep the tough emotions at bay. (I was that busy, busy, busy woman. Unnecessarily stacking my schedule to keep my mind occupied and not dealing with necessary things is something I still have to guard against.)
- ☐ You won't admit the truth to yourself.
- ☐ You have stopped dreaming, planning, or even hoping.

Avoidance will eventually work itself into your actions. The following is what it looks like when it becomes actions and what areas it affects.

To give some structure, these are the areas to evaluate for avoidance:

Relationships, Spiritual Health, Physical Health, Mental Health, Personal Finances, Personal Goals—Career, Professional Development. Note that some avoidances affect all areas of your life.

Unhealthy External Avoidance

- ☐ Avoiding any type of confrontation with a human. *(Relationships.)*
- ☐ Avoiding having a challenging conversation with a boss, superior, pastor, leader, or mentor. These have you in a subordinate role, which can be particularly taxing as the outcome may hurt you. *(Relationships/ Career.)*
- ☐ An estranged family member or friend. *(Relationships.)*
- ☐ Avoiding telling the truth to a spouse, loved one, family member, friend, coworker, boss, or even a stranger. These are lies of omission/self-preservation. We don't trust enough to be vulnerable, so we control the image others have of us. We create a fictional persona that we feel makes us acceptable. These lies usually don't stay hidden. If we do manage to keep them secret, we remain a shell of who we could be. (*This one affects all areas.)*
- ☐ You don't own past mistakes without justifying why the mistakes happened. As opposed to just owning your mistakes and trusting that who you are now speaks for itself! *(Personal Goals /Relationships / Spiritual Health.)*
- ☐ You avoid giving true forgiveness to someone who hurt or harmed you. *(Relationships.)*
- ☐ Avoiding the potential for new dating relationships or even refusing to put yourself out there at all. *(Relationships.)*
- ☐ Staying in an unhealthy/toxic friendship, relationship, or marriage. *(Relationships.)*
- ☐ Not going places you have been invited to or making plans and then backing out or canceling at the last minute or making excuses to not hang out with friends. *(Relationships.)*

- ☐ Not staying in touch with friends and family—not returning phone calls or texts, visiting, taking time for connection. *(Relationships.)*
- ☐ Avoiding having close friends with whom you can be your most genuine self, vulnerable and honest—if your significant other or your parent is the only close friend in your life, you should explore why. *(Relationships.)*
- ☐ Not attending social gatherings or events when there is no valid reason not to go. *(Relationships.)*
- ☐ You avoid going to certain places because of fear of what you look like, e.g., the beach, the gym, sports events, formal events, some type of adventure activity like hiking or swimming. *(Relationships, Physical Health.)*
- ☐ You avoid having people over to your home. *(Relationships.)*
- ☐ Avoiding sleeping overnight anywhere other than your home. It would take an act of Congress for you to sleep anywhere but your bed! *(Relationships, Personal Goals, Career.)*
- ☐ Avoidance of regular, consistent chores in the home (laundry, dishes, vacuum, sweeping, picking up, etc.) *(This can affect all areas of your life.)*
- ☐ Refusing to get rid of things you haven't used in many years or no longer serve a purpose / holding on to things / hoarding. *(This can affect all areas of your life.)*

Phase Five: Avoidance

- ☐ Avoiding personal organization—whether in the workplace, home life, cleaning out your car, cleaning out the junk drawers, closets, etc. *(This can affect all areas of your life.)*
- ☐ Avoiding healthy eating / lifestyle changes *(This can affect all areas of your life.)*
- ☐ Avoiding exercise *(This can affect not just your overall health but all areas of your life.)*
- ☐ Avoiding going back to college, obtaining that certification, furthering a skill in the workplace, learning a new hobby, or developing other skills in a hobby you already love. You won't consider applying for a new job, exploring a new career option, taking a risk so you can ultimately have that dream job or own your own business. *(Personal Goals, Personal Finances, Career.)*
- ☐ You write a to-do list or set up a calendar or task but end up avoiding it because it's too daunting or overwhelming. *(This can affect all areas of your life.)*
- ☐ Not using your voice for good, not being vulnerable, and sharing your pain for a purpose—you basically stay silent when, in reality, you have something to offer to this world. *(Relationships, Personal Goals.)*
- ☐ Not taking care of your mental health (putting off going to therapy, seeking counsel/guidance for mental health problems or stress, seeing a doctor for mental health medication, etc.). *(This can affect all areas of your life.)*
- ☐ Not taking care of your physical health (putting off or avoiding doctor visits, checkups, much-needed medical tests, dental visits, eye appointments, or hearing appointments). *(This can affect all areas of your life.)*
- ☐ Avoiding God, prayer, Bible reading, growing in your faith. *(Spiritual Health, Relationships.)*

- ☐ Not going to church, getting connected to a church body, or a spiritual/faith-based group, volunteering, or serving in a church setting. *(Spiritual Health, Relationships.)*
- ☐ Avoidance of paperwork or a task that you are not confident in or don't like doing. *(Personal Goals, Personal Finances.)*
- ☐ You avoid paying past bills/collections, sticking to a budget, paying off debt. *(Personal Finances, Personal Goals, Career.)*
- ☐ Since you don't ask for help, you attempt "to do it all" or be "superwoman," "super mom," "super dad," or "superman." *(This will affect all areas of life.)*
- ☐ Avoidance of eating in public or with large groups of people. *(Relationships, Personal Goals.)*
- ☐ Staying busy or distracted so you can justify why you have been avoiding the above list. *(This affects all areas of your life.)*
- ☐ You are physically sick. What's the fear? There is no fear here. Physical illness happens after intrusive fearful thoughts are allowed to flow unmitigated and unrestrained. Cortisol is your body's primary stress hormone, designed to work with the parts of your brain that deal with the healthy state of your body. (Think about how that can malfunction when you live with constant fearful thoughts.) Fear makes itself known in anxiety, depression, headaches, heart disease, memory and concentration, digestion issues, sleeplessness, weight gain, and a whole host of other things that you don't recognize.

After reading this list, is there anything you are avoiding that wasn't mentioned above? Write it here.

Now that you have identified the areas you avoid, Phase Three addresses the root of your avoidance.

Are you ready? Be brave. This will help you.

Phase Six

The Mind Trap

"Every avoidance behavior has a root, and that root is fear."
— Vera

Reread the above statement. Let it sink in. Don't think you have any fear? Everyone has fear. Some of it is healthy self-preservation. That kind of fear keeps us from stepping onto the highway when cars are rushing toward us.

But there is an unhealthy fear that can rule and ruin your life. Unhealthy fear is insidious, creeping in slowly and taking over every part of your life until fear becomes your normal processor. And, sometimes, when you've lived with fear navigating all your thoughts, words, and actions long enough, you no longer recognize the torment of it until it's gone.

Again, we go to the Scriptures to show us humanity's first introduction to fear.

> *"But the Lord God called to the man, 'Where are you?' He answered, 'I heard you in the garden, and I was afraid because I was naked; so I hid'"* (Genesis 3:9–10 NIV).

Note also, in verses 11 and 12, that Adam blames his avoidance on his wife once discovered. That avoidance leads to more avoidance, one of responsibility.

> *"And he said, 'Who told you that you were naked? Have you eaten from the tree that I commanded you not to eat from?' The man said, 'The woman you put here with me—she gave me some fruit from the tree, and I ate it'"* (NIV).

And don't we do that? We blame others, or circumstances, to justify not taking responsibility. When ultimately, it is our responsibility to handle our own lives.

In a client interview, Michelle lays avoidance out like this:

> *"I put it* [her trauma] *in this little bitty box—in the back of my mind. But even though I was ignoring it, it was popping out in different areas of my life. I remember I dealt with a lot of depression and anxiety. I would have panic attacks. When I was a teenager, I started cutting myself. And even when I remember now, like, I'm saying this, but even as I was a little older, I would see myself driving off the road when I started driving. It was very much like—I always had control of it—I never wanted to die, but there was also that thought that maybe this would shut it off. Maybe that's why I cut myself because I felt like, okay, if I could focus on this pain, then I won't have to focus on my emotional pain. And then, once I got into high school, I started drinking.*
>
> *And a big thing that I had to face up to was* ***my*** *actions—going through BFA helped me face that. Okay, yes, I was abused, and things happened to me, but I also made a lot of choices on my own that* [her dad] *had nothing to do with. And I had to face up to that, you know, and really*

> *be real with myself, and be like okay, I was abused, and these are the characteristics I got from it. You know, like the depression, the codependence, stuff like that. But then I had to take the reins and be like, okay, I have to take control of this. I can't be a victim anymore. I'm not in that abusive situation anymore; I haven't been in that situation since I was a young teen. I've been separated from it.* ***And the stuff that I've done since then has been my own choice.****"*

It takes a new level of maturity, understanding, and courage to own the choices we make after traumatic experiences. But with that owning comes healing.

As a therapist, I talk about fear nearly every day. Typically, when someone reaches out for counseling, they will report symptoms or current problems such as anxiety, depression, stress, grief, or family stressors. Rarely is the word fear mentioned first.

How do I describe fear to my clients? I tell them fear is both a feeling and behavior.

If you have ever experienced fear at any level, you know what I mean. And if you examine this a little deeper, you probably recall what you avoided because of that fear. I want to tell you a story about my fear of having a hard conversation with my biological father. But first, I want to get your mind thinking about the different forms fear may take. Which of these do you identify as your behaviors?

- ☐ You find yourself striving in vain for an impossible-to-achieve standard of perfection. Real problem? You are afraid of criticism, failure, and rejection.
- ☐ You settle. Why? It's a lack of confidence, faith, and understanding of your identity in Christ.
- ☐ You say yes when you mean no. Real problem? You are afraid to disappoint people or be rejected if you don't say yes.
- ☐ You say no when you mean yes. Why? You are afraid to take risks, fail, fear what people will think of you, or fear rejection.
- ☐ You numb yourself with escape-like behaviors, e.g., gambling, excessive drinking, shopping, binge-watching TV, etc. What is the fear here? You are afraid to be quiet with yourself, face inner demons head-on, and heal from the core.
- ☐ You procrastinate. What fears are lurking? The fear of putting yourself out there. It's safer for you to stand on the sidelines.
- ☐ You become emotionally paralyzed. What is the real fear? You are stuck and are terrified of the uncertainty of future outcomes.
- ☐ You are a control freak. Why? You are so afraid of the unknown that you want to control everything and everyone so that the outcome is one that you can handle. The result may be repeatedly toxic or not move you out of a destructive cycle, but it is predictable. And the expected outcome, no surprises, therefore no outcome the controller is not equipped to handle. You trust yourself and your abilities too much. Your way isn't the only way. You're not the only one for the job.
- ☐ You muzzle yourself. Real problem? You don't speak up because you are afraid of the response, possible rejection, or loss.

That Hard Conversation with John

I mentioned earlier that I was the queen of avoidance, especially with difficult and emotional conversations. It was something woven into me from as far back as I can remember.

What I conjured in my mind isn't what happened in the end.

Tesa, my momma, is about the sweetest Southern woman on the bayou. To know her is to love her. She has not a mean bone in her body. I am approaching forty years old at this writing, and I can tell you I have never seen this woman raise her voice, lose her patience, or be mean to anyone. Pretty impressive, right? Yeah, it is, but it came at a cost. How so?

For one, I didn't see her stand up for herself, ever. I also didn't see her confront complicated situations or even discuss them. Instead, she just chose to be happy, present, help others, and stay busy being a mother and educator.

With my biological father not being involved in my upbringing, avoiding uncomfortable situations or conversations was easy. My mother never spoke ill of him and kept everything positive, so I learned very young to just focus on the one acceptable emotion—being happy.

How did that work for me? Well, in the ways that I am like my mother, it worked well for me. But in the areas that I am opposite my mother, "being happy" just didn't get the job done. Let me explain.

To know me is to know that I am a curious person. I want to know the meaning of things. I want to understand where emotions originate. I want to see the purpose behind things and the reason they exist. I just want to know. I love knowledge, and I love to understand why people do what they do. Wonder why I picked the profession I did?

So naturally throughout my childhood I always wondered why my biological father just walked away from my twin sister and me. Of course, I knew I didn't have the whole story, but what I did know from my mother was her version of events that sprawled out over those early years of my life and the life of my twin sister. It was the "happy" version. The "I'm okay, you're okay, we are all okay" version. I did not doubt that she and my family loved me. But she gave me the friendly version—the version that protected my sister and me.

I would sometimes envision and play out a dramatic conversation with my biological father throughout my life—the ultimate confrontation. The "let me tell you how I feel" kinda confrontation in which he, so moved with what I say, sobs uncontrollably. Too many Hallmark movies, I know.

I thought maybe there were some other parts of the story my mom had left out and that one day he would have a perfect reason as to why he walked away.

After I became a mother of my own, I didn't understand how a mother or father could walk out of their children's lives when they were absolutely capable of raising a child. I became angered at the thought of it. I am not referring to the selfless act of adoption in critical situations—I didn't feel I fell into that category. I am not referring to the mother or father who tirelessly fights to be involved in their child's life after a divorce or custody dispute. I am talking about the parent that just walks away and starts an entirely new life as though they do not have existing children.

I looked at my precious, brown-eyed baby boy and wondered how in the world could I ever do anything but the best for him. And then, I looked at my husband, who was on his A-game from the moment our son was born. I knew Seth would never walk away. Just as I knew there was nothing Seth wouldn't do to fight for our son and make him feel secure. Watching my husband step into his role of fatherhood was so beautiful to watch but also confused me on a personal level.

During these moments of early parenthood, Seth and I would have conversations about my biological father and the many questions I still had. Seth would often encourage me to have a conversation with John, but how would I do that?

Should I just pick up the phone and say, "Hey, it's your oldest daughter, Vera, and I have quite some questions for you?" Ummm, that was awkward and weird! Should I just send him a Facebook message and say, "Hey, how are you…I have a lot of questions for you?" Wait, he didn't even have social media. So, that wasn't an option. It was so awkward and uncomfortable to even think about just starting the process of trying to have a conversation—it was just easier to avoid.

In reality, I wished, hoped, dreamed that he would find me, that he would just come to me. Why did I have to go to him? Wasn't he also avoiding me? Maybe I genetically inherited my avoidance from him. That's where it came from, after all. Ha!

Avoidance is just easier most of the time—I mean all of the time.

I came up with so many reasons why I didn't need to go to him first. Any person who has felt rejected, unwanted, or discounted by a parent, loved one, or friend can identify with this train of thought.

Why me? Why do I need to be the "bigger person" and go to you? Were you not the parent who chose to walk away? It wasn't me. You left me—I didn't leave you first.

And that is the truth. It wasn't me who started it. But it was me that was actively continuing what my biological father started. Ouch.

I was actively avoiding what he started, so how was I any different? The very things I hated—abandonment, avoidance, rejection, the silent treatment—I was doing! Why was I doing them? Because I was afraid. So, I just hid from him.

I was afraid of being rejected again, not being loved or accepted, not being good enough, or not being heard and understood. And I feared the failure of losing the relationships I already had by opening the door to new ones I had never had.

Do you know how many of these fears came true? None of them. Were there painful moments? Yes, but not debilitating. Instead, it was more like the type of pain one associates with using a stiff leg muscle. The hurt diminishes as the use becomes consistent until the pain is a memory and no longer hindering one's stride.

The Bible talks about spiritual senses being strengthened by use.

> *"But strong meat belongeth to them that are of full age, even those who by reason of use have their senses exercised to discern both good and evil."* (Hebrews 5:14 KJV)

It's the same with our "emotional senses." We get stronger, healthier, and more capable of facing and dealing with our emotional wounds by—you guessed it—dealing with our emotional wounds.

Even though fear is the root of avoidance, you will benefit from anxiety having a phase of its own. So, move into the next phase and work it with this one.

Phase Seven

What I Believe Is What I Do

"What I believe is not what I say I believe; what I believe is what I do."
— Donald Miller

In south Louisiana, onions, bell peppers, and celery are called the holy trinity. Once you've had them in your food, you don't want anything else! You get stuck on the taste. Mmmm, so good.

The mind can become stuck in a trinity of its own, an unholy one. This combo is named fear, worry, and anxiety. Ugh, not so good.

What is anxiety? If you have experienced anxiety, I probably don't even have to explain it—you just know the feeling. You know the mental struggle, the oppressive weight, the suffocating blanket of some nameless enemy that wants to take you out in the most gruesome of ways—a mental meltdown.

According to the American Psychological Association, anxiety is *"an emotion characterized by feelings of tension, worried thoughts, and physical changes like increased blood pressure.*

People with anxiety disorders usually have recurring intrusive thoughts or concerns. They may avoid certain situations out of worry. They may also have physical symptoms such as sweating, trembling, dizziness, or a rapid heartbeat."

Does that sound about right? Or perhaps, for you, it sounds exactly right. From the above definition, we can determine that anxiety can and does affect us mentally and physically. Do you really have time for that? I know I don't, and if my clients are predictive of the consensus, neither do you.

Christians are not immune to anxiety or depression. One main problem in Christian circles is that anxiety is considered a spiritual problem—like a lack of faith. I can say with certainty this is not always the case.

Anxiety is rooted in fear. Anxiety is a symptom of underlying negative core beliefs about oneself, others, or the world around one

Root Systems

What are core beliefs? Core beliefs are typically all-or-nothing statements that are rigid or overgeneralized views about yourself, others, or how the world "works"; in particular, they are unhealthy or negative. It's an unhealthy mental root system.

If you consistently experience a pervasive negative thinking pattern (this means an unwelcome influence on your thoughts), then that is a sign of internal negative core beliefs.

Core beliefs generally develop at an early age through adolescence—they can be shaped by others (parents, teachers, coaches, peers), events in our lives (traumatic and successful), and genetics / biological vulnerability (intelligence, temperament, specific skills or lack thereof).

What are your thoughts saying to you about yourself? Think about your self-thoughts and find the ones that resonate with you.

DEFECTIVENESS

- ☐ I'm not good enough.
- ☐ I can't get anything right.
- ☐ I'm nothing.
- ☐ I'm stupid.
- ☐ I'm insignificant.
- ☐ I've done things wrong.
- ☐ I'm a failure.
- ☐ I'm unattractive (ugly, fat, etc.).
- ☐ I don't deserve anything good.
- ☐ There is something wrong with me.

ABANDONMENT

- ☐ People I love will leave me.
- ☐ I will be abandoned if I love or care for something/someone.
- ☐ I am unimportant.
- ☐ If I assert myself, people will leave me.
- ☐ I can't be happy if I'm on my own.
- ☐ My partner is no longer interested in me.
- ☐ I am bound to be rejected, abandoned, or alone.

UNLOVABLE

- ☐ I'm not lovable.
- ☐ I'm always left out.
- ☐ I am alone.
- ☐ Nobody loves me.
- ☐ Nobody wants me.
- ☐ I am bound to be rejected.
- ☐ I don't fit in anywhere.
- ☐ I don't matter.
- ☐ I'm not as good as other people.

HELPLESSNESS

- ☐ I am helpless, powerless.
- ☐ I am out of control.
- ☐ I must have control to be okay.
- ☐ I am weak.
- ☐ I am trapped.
- ☐ I am needy.
- ☐ I am unsuccessful.
- ☐ I am trapped and can't escape.
- ☐ I can't do it.
- ☐ I can't say no.
- ☐ If I experience emotions, I will lose control.
- ☐ I can't change.

ENTITLEMENT

- ☐ If people don't respect me, I can't stand it.
- ☐ If I don't excel, then I'll just end up ordinary.
- ☐ Other people should satisfy my needs.
- ☐ People have no right to criticize me.
- ☐ Other people don't deserve the good things they get.
- ☐ People don't understand/get me because I am (special, brilliant, etc.).

CARETAKING

- ☐ It's not okay to ask for help.
- ☐ I have to do everything perfectly.
- ☐ I'm responsible for everyone and everything.
- ☐ My needs are not important.
- ☐ I shouldn't spend time taking care of myself.
- ☐ When I see that others need help, I have to help them.
- ☐ I am only worthwhile if I'm helping other people.
- ☐ If I express negative feelings in a relationship, terrible things will happen.

Breaking Free From Anxiety

The opposite of anxiety is not faith; it's ACTION. We break free of the bondage of fear and anxiety by becoming a person of ACTION.

When it comes to anxiety, there are two options.

Option 1: Choose to continue to believe the negative thoughts that come your way due to unhealthy core beliefs about yourself, others, and the world around you. This, by the way, causes you to stay stuck in anxious, chaotic thinking. Or,

Option 2: Choose the path of ACTION.

The answer is—you guessed it—we don't settle for less than action.

The Bible tells us that our mental wellbeing is an important component to living a life of peace. In Philippians 4:6–7 the Scripture instructs us:

> *"Do not be anxious about anything, but in every situation, by prayer and petition, with thanksgiving, present your requests to God. And the peace of God, which transcends all understanding, will guard your hearts and your minds in Christ Jesus."*

Well, that's pretty plain, right? Then the next two verses give more ACTION. Verses 8 and 9 say:

> *"Finally, brothers and sisters, whatever is true, whatever is noble, whatever is right, whatever is pure, whatever is lovely, whatever is admirable—if anything is excellent or praiseworthy—think about such things. Whatever you have learned or received or heard from me or seen in me—put it into practice. And the God of peace will be with you."*

That was Paul speaking to the church in Philippi. Now, look at what he wrote about himself to the people in Corinth. This is an interesting insight into how a leader manages a personal, persistent struggle. In 2 Corinthians 12:7–10, beginning with the end of verse 7, Paul says,

> *"I was given a thorn in my flesh, a messenger of Satan, to torment me.*
>
> *Three times I pleaded with the Lord to take it away from me. But he said to me, 'My grace is sufficient for you, for my power is made perfect in weakness.'*
>
> *Therefore, I will boast all the more gladly about my weaknesses, so that Christ's power may rest on me. That is why, for Christ's sake, I delight in weaknesses, in insults, in hardships, in persecutions, in difficulties. For when I am weak, then I am strong."*

What was he pleading to God to take away? Scripture doesn't say specifically. Some biblical scholars believe the "thorn in the flesh" may have been a physical problem such as defective eyesight, a lisp, epilepsy, or recurrent malaria. Or perhaps it was spiritual—a temptation, such as lust, which can take the form of excessive desire for things or of sexual immorality. It may have even been an individual or group who continually harassed Paul, and he struggled to respond with a pure heart.

In any case, it was bothersome to him. But instead of removing the "thorn," God assured Paul that his grace and strength would be sufficient for Paul to bear it. So, am I telling you that there may be things you will never overcome? I rarely use the absolute of never in the context of mental and emotional healing. What I am telling you is that Paul's "thorn in the flesh" destroyed his pride and kept him dependent on divine power. Therefore, although unpleasant, Paul regarded the "thorn" as an AID rather than a handicap. His dependence on God made that thorn manageable. Paul controlled it through his faith in God.

When it comes to anxious thoughts, those absolutely can and should be managed. By you.

This diagram explains an unhealthy thought cycle. Fear communicates unhealthy messages. It tells us to avoid. It keeps us stuck in a cycle of chaos.

According to clinical Neuropsychologist, Dr. Michelle Bengtson, 7.3 percent of the world's population, about one in thirteen people, suffers from an anxiety disorder. Anxiety is, in the counselors' world, the common cold of mental illness.[18] Keep in mind this is 7.3 percent of diagnosed cases, so the percentages are higher because of the unreported cases.

Our brains are the processors of our thoughts, and our thoughts have the power to alter our neuropathways. This alteration means an unhealthy change when those thoughts are consistently negative and fearful. That change, in turn, produces a whole host of problems and challenges in every part of your life.

Research has proven that 91 percent of what we worry about never happens. (Penn State University Research). But that doesn't mean that it's okay to allow anxious thoughts to run unchecked through our minds. Thoughts will always trigger a response. You get to decide what your thoughts trigger, not if they trigger. Choose wisely and healthily.

Why are these statistics significant to you? They are significant because it's essential you know you are not alone. When we know that others have faced that giant and conquered it, we can also. We can look at the strategies proven to work and plan a strategy to go after our peace. Yes, you read that right.

Fear creates inaction, a paralysis of sorts. Oh, we are busy, busy, busy, all right. But it is treadmill running—movement that takes you nowhere—doing but getting nothing of importance done.

---

18 https://drmichellebengtson.com/where-do-anxiety-worry-and-fear-come-from/

I avoid doing something that needs doing, but I am too uncomfortable to do it. So instead, I engage in stalling, putting it off, procrastinating until the last minute or after the said deadline. When I engage in avoidance, I engage in a behavior or behaviors to replace the thing I should be doing.

What might it look like when we are "busy" avoiding? It may look like:

- ★ Staying busy — packing that schedule with tasks, places to go, people to see, helping others.
- ★ Escaping by engaging in excessive screen time — television, movies, social media scrolling, YouTube watching, app games, video games.
- ★ Excessive cleaning/organizing/planning — instead of doing the things that really need to get done.
- ★ Excessive sleep/lying around — whether that be staying in bed or lying on the couch.

Have you recognized yourself? Yes? Write it down; you will address it in Chapter Two.

1 Samuel chapter 17 verse 35, gives the account of David defending the sheep in his care. David says, *"I went after it, struck it, and rescued the sheep from its mouth. Then, when it turned on me, I seized it by its hair, struck it, and killed it."*

I know, I know. You don't own any sheep. But what is in your care? Your mind. Your thoughts. If you don't care for your mind, it will turn on you. When you don't control your thoughts, they control you. A human mind is a complex place. It's dangerous to go there unarmed. But God.

The Scripture teaches us that God has equipped us.

> *"For God has not given us a spirit of fear, but of power and of love and of a sound mind"* (2 Timothy 1:7).

The reference to "sound mind" is of a filter. What is the job of a filter? A filter removes impurities. I suggest you pause and let that rattle around your thought processes for a minute, grasp the significance of it.

Ephesians 6:8–18 discusses the whole armor of God. This armor comes complete with a sword, shield, and helmet. God has given you tools for your protection; as David did, you, too, can go after what is holding your mind hostage, hit it hard, and rescue yourself from the paralysis of avoidance.

Hang around for the how-to tools given in Chapter Two of this book. But don't go there just yet, you have a bit more to do here.

I've told you about some of my fears now, let's explore yours. What? Did you think you wouldn't have to address yours? *sigh* You better get a snack or put on your comfort clothes because this may get a bit rough. Don't lose hope though, your Chapter Two is coming, and it will get better.

Fears Associated with Avoidance. (Why we justify our unhealthy avoidance.) Use this as a self-evaluation. Place a check in the boxes that identify your fear-avoidance patterns—you will be working on these. Reminder: what we don't identify, we won't change, control, or eliminate.

- ☐ The fear of failing—even in the slightest way
- ☐ The embarrassment that comes with feeling like you failed and the possibility that someone will judge you or think differently of you
- ☐ The fear of not being able to control your emotions if you do confront someone or stand up for yourself—which also leads to more embarrassment or shame.

In the words of a dear friend, "I get tongue-tied like Moses when he was about to talk to Pharaoh—I never get out what I want to say, and then I start crying! I don't want to recreate those situations again, so I just avoid them!"

- ☐ The fear that your voice isn't heard or doesn't matter or isn't valued.
- ☐ The fear of you still getting the blame or something being "all your fault" so you don't bring up that hard conversation.
- ☐ The fear that the emotions of grief are just too powerful, and you won't survive processing them.

- ☐ The fear of losing control or not being in control of yourself: can include your emotions, thoughts of yourself or others, your behaviors, and the behaviors of others.
- ☐ The fear of not having enough—whether that is money, security, safety, food, some type of materialistic item.

Not trying is the failure part. Making a mistake, giving it your best attempt, putting yourself out there, and not getting the results you want—all of that is still a win. What's not a win is staying stuck and just not even attempting. While writing this book, I saw a Netflix documentary called *7 Yards*—featuring the life of Chris Norton,[19] who developed paraplegia after a college football injury.

Chris has beat so many odds and is continuing to do so. His story is beyond encouraging, but my favorite line from his interview came at the documentary's end.

He said, "When I hear people say they can't, it really means they won't. Anything is possible."

When telling his story concerning his recovery from a sports injury, James Clear, author of *Atomic Habits*, wrote: "…I knew that if things were going to improve, I was the one responsible for making it happen."[20]

I want to encourage you to do the very thing of which you are afraid. Do the work because anything is possible. At the very least, you are worth that much.

---

19 https://chrisnorton.org/about/

20 *Atomic Habits: An Easy & Proven Way to Build Good Habits & Break Bad Ones* Clear, James, Avery, 2018.

Phase Seven: What I Believe Is What I Do

"Then David said to Solomon his son, 'Be strong and courageous and do it. Do not be afraid and do not be dismayed, for the Lord God, even my God, is with you. He will not leave you or forsake you, until all the work for the service of the house of the Lord is finished'"

(1 Chronicles 28:20)

Phase Eight

Stop Circling The Drain

"Chaos, when left alone, tends to multiply."
— Stephen Hawking

Even though we know all the things that made us who we are today, that doesn't immediately take us out of patterns and processes. There is no pixie dust available to sprinkle on our lives and magically create new coping strategies and healing to our wounded souls.

Addiction cannot be lectured away or prayed away. Taking responsibility by learning the tools to overcome the addiction—what I call the cycle of chaos—or the negative mindset and using the tools you learned are key to changing behaviors leading to a life of peace, productivity, and purpose.

When we do our part, God does the rest. A renewed mind happens under the guidance and direction of the Holy Spirit.

A licensed marriage and family therapist, Marnie C. Ferree, explains emotional healing and growth this way:

> *"Instead of delivering, I believe God blesses and empowers people with the intelligence and knowledge to address the problems in their lives. God has equipped human creation with the capability to split the atom, to travel to the moon, to build amazing structures and to cure diseases. It is insufficient—and indeed, I believe, wrong—to sit back and trust God to heal cancer or heart disease or addiction and do nothing to help yourself by taking advantage of the knowledge and tools available in treating those diseases."*

I agree with Marnie. No one is beyond hope, and everyone deals with toxic thoughts and the resulting unwanted results. The apostle Paul shared his struggle with unwanted behaviors when he describes, in Romans 7:15–25, his battle with doing those things he doesn't want to do and not doing those things he wants to do. Paul confesses that he doesn't understand himself and that he *hates* what he does! We can relate, Paul.

Whew! It's like Paul wrote about us, right? Instead of that being a negative thing, it's a hopeful one. Why? Because he ends that passage of Scripture with the encouraging promise that changing our lives is doable through Jesus.

Why are we so unsuccessful at stopping what Paul discusses in Romans chapter 7, *"doing what I do not want to do"*?

The answer lies in the disease concept of addiction and the "law of the mind."

Addiction

Dr. Patrick Carnes, author of *The Betrayal Bond*, has given a simple definition of addiction, *"Addiction is having a pathological relationship with a mood-altering substance or behavior."*[21]

Huh. A pathological relationship with something? Yes, it's an unhealthy habitual, maladaptive, and compulsive

---

21 *The Betrayal Bond: Breaking Free of Exploitive Relationships* Carnes, Patrick J., Health Communications, Inc., 1997, 2019.

habit—something that never produces good and life-giving results.

We accept that alcohol and drugs become addictive; after all, those are substances taken into our bodies. There is an obvious physiological chemical reaction that occurs when we consume drugs or alcohol. But having sex, gambling, overeating, undereating, or toxic relationships don't necessarily involve ingesting a chemical. How do such behaviors become addictions?

What makes a behavior fit into the definition of addiction? The answers are found in the four characteristics of the cycle of chaos.

It is hard to identify the exact point when a behavior crosses the line into being an addiction, but most everyone can pinpoint a time in their life where the discomforts of their life became too intense to handle.

In his book *Atomic Habits*, James Clear gives us a life interpretation of what the apostle Paul calls "the law of the mind" and what I call the cycle of chaos. Clear wrote:

> *"Negative thoughts compound. The more you think of yourself as worthless, stupid, or ugly, the more you condition yourself to interpret life that way. You get trapped in a thought loop. The same is true for how you think about others. Once you fall into the habit of seeing people as angry, unjust, or selfish, you see those kind of people everywhere."*

In those few short sentences, Clear identifies what I, as a therapist, address with all my clients—thoughts and perceptions and the resulting actions that come with them.

Phase Eight: Stop Circling The Drain

Let's analyze your thought patterns for a moment. Your mindset has a powerful way of either keeping you out of chaotic cycles or putting you right back in them. The negative mind says things like:

- "I am not enough."
- "I'll never overcome this addiction."
- "I can't leave this relationship."
- "I am angry that God would allow this to happen to me!"
- "Why is this my reality—I guess this is my punishment for my past."
- "I am better off dead."
- "I have caused too much pain in people's lives."
- "The guilt I carry will never go away!"
- "That relationship will never be healed."
- "I will never get ahead!"
- "This life is hopeless."

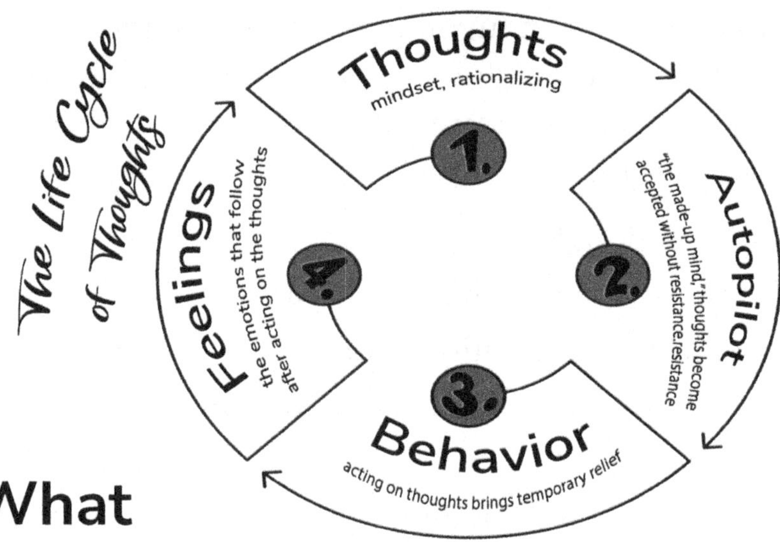

What are your thoughts telling you?

What is autopilot as it relates to a cycle of chaos? It is a psychological automatic response that occurs in which the person no longer is consciously driving their thoughts on a particular event, circumstance, or person; instead their mind drives them toward an action or behavior that is unhealthy. This is where you no longer rationalize why something may not be a "good idea," but you believe that thought to be absolute truth and something you must act on.

For example, if I am driving a car at seventy miles per hour, I have to consciously keep my foot steady on the accelerator to maintain the speed I want to go. But, if I put it on autopilot, then I no longer need to focus on keeping the accelerator pressure steady. The decision has shifted from conscious to unconscious.

Our thoughts, in turn, trigger behaviors and reactions. Chaotic behavior looks something like:

- ❖ losing your temper and taking out your anger on loved ones or friends
- ❖ letting your mouth run and not knowing when to stop
- ❖ drinking or smoking too much, abusing prescription pills, smoking pot, using whatever type of drug provides you temporary comfort and relief
- ❖ blaming God for your traumas or hardships and refusing to pray or attend church
- ❖ shutting people out of your life and becoming your own therapist
- ❖ staying in toxic relationships
- ❖ allowing people to use you
- ❖ gossiping about others
- ❖ using pornography
- ❖ controlling every situation
- ❖ overeating and undereating

What else? Write it here.

Did you pass over the above without evaluating yourself? If so, go back and evaluate. Take just one thing that never ends well and pick it apart.

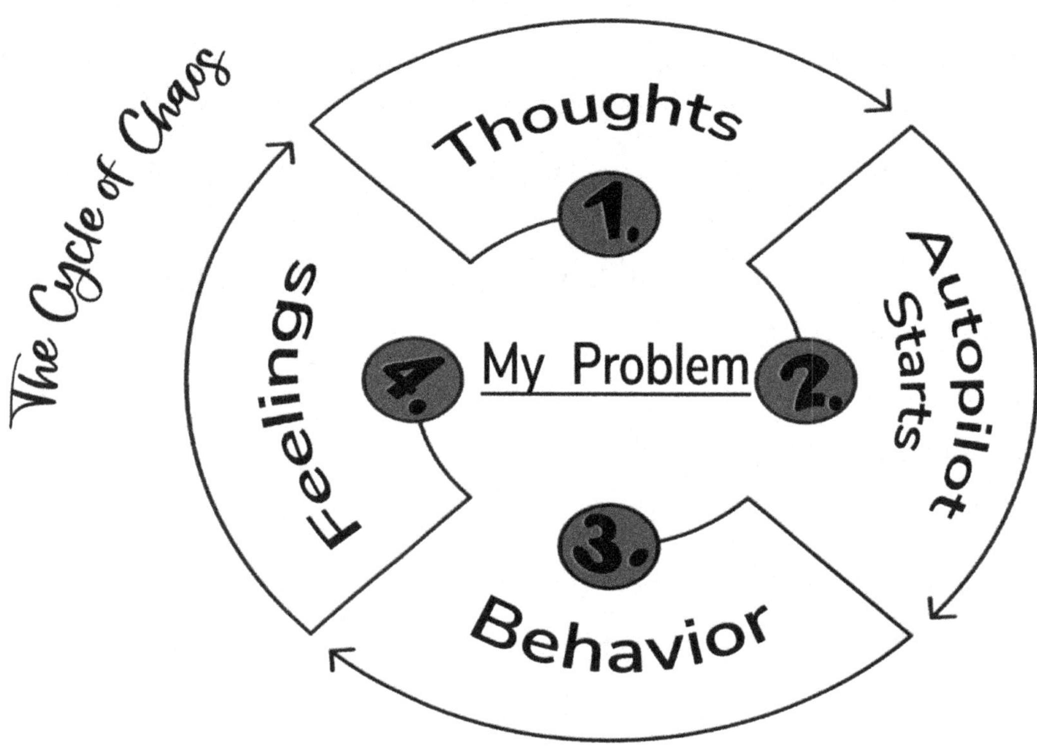

Don't let that wheel of despair rattle around in your head, you'll have an opportunity to change that cycle in your Chapter Two. How about if I go first by sharing a problem, people pleasing, that I work hard to keep in check.

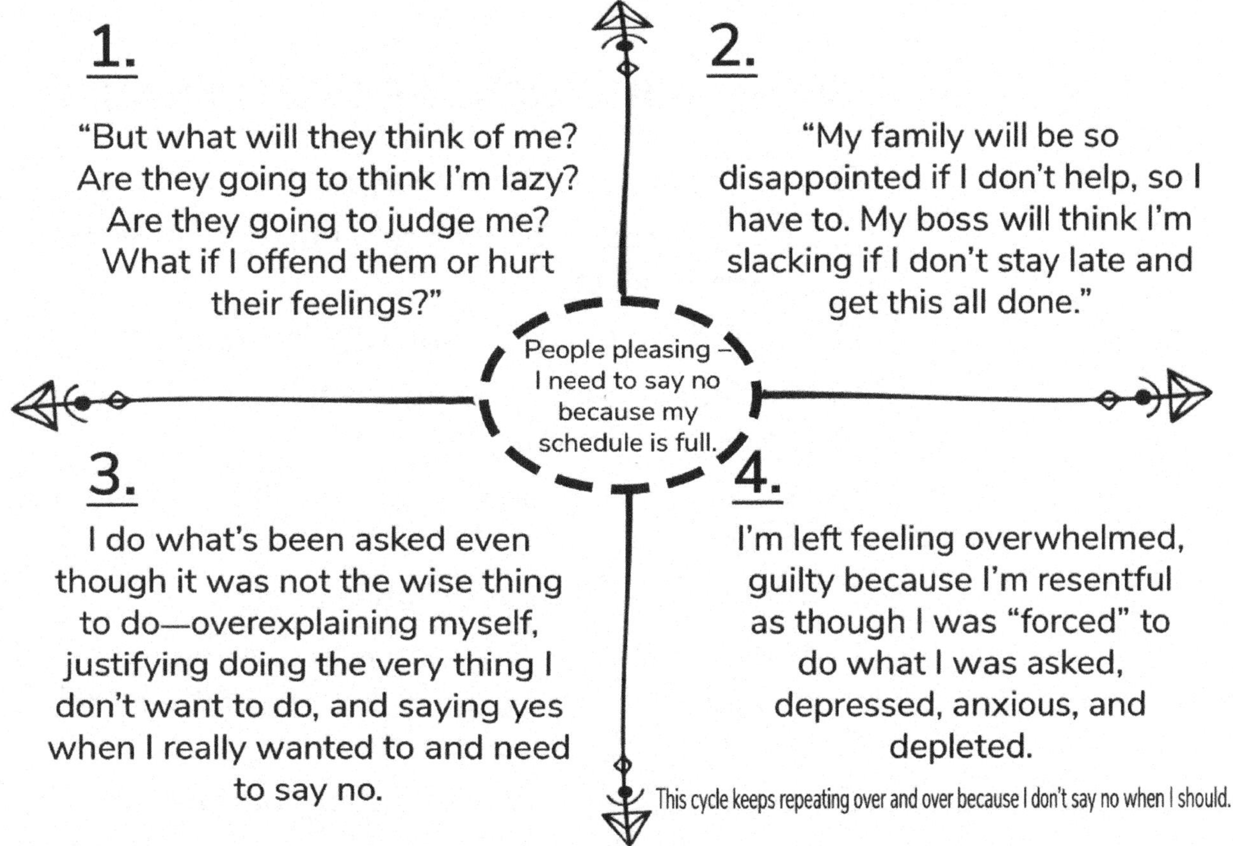

First, let me share that people pleasing is not a psychological diagnosis but, when unaddressed for prolonged periods, leads to anxiety, depression, codependency (also known as *dependent personality disorder*), or avoidant personality disorder.

How did I recognize I was a people pleaser? Well, at one time or another, I have checked all the boxes listed on this page. I think that's a pretty good indicator.

I like to say I'm in a cycle of success rather than a cycle of chaos, sort of a post people pleaser. But sometimes triggers happen, and I find myself putting a hard stop midway through a cycle of chaos. So, I understand the struggle to change thinking patterns.

Now it's your turn to check or not check the boxes.

SIGNS YOU ARE A PEOPLE PLEASER

- ☐ You find it very hard to say no.
- ☐ You are preoccupied or consumed with what others think of you.
- ☐ You feel guilty when you tell others no.
- ☐ You fear if you say no, then others will think you are selfish or mean.
- ☐ You say yes to things you don't like or don't want to do.
- ☐ You struggle with low self-esteem.
- ☐ You genuinely want people to like you. To avoid making enemies you feel doing for others will earn or keep their approval.
- ☐ "I'm sorry" often comes out of your mouth, especially if others seem upset that things didn't go their way.
- ☐ You take the blame even when it's not your fault.
- ☐ You never have free time because you are always doing things for other people. (This one screams my name!)
- ☐ You neglect or sacrifice your own needs to do something for others.
- ☐ You go along or pretend to agree with people even though you really disagree or feel differently.

Now that wasn't so hard, right? Okay, it might have been hard, but you are the bravest!

What causes people pleasing? Well, poor self-esteem and self-worth, insecurity, a personal struggle with perfectionism, and past hurtful or traumatic experiences where, for example, we stood up for ourselves, and it ended badly.

What are the effects of being a people pleaser? This question is a tricky thing. Why? Because the people pleasers' greatest strengths—kindness and their loving and generous hearts—are their weaknesses as well.

As you might guess, those attributes leave us vulnerable and easy targets for those who take advantage of others. Since everyone is so used to having our yes, they don't recognize we are overwhelmed or overworked. And truthfully, it's not the responsibility of others to mind our boundaries. It's ours.

Therefore, we are left feeling like no one sees us or checks on us. We are only good for what we can give or do for someone else.

I can't even begin to tell you how many times I cried to my husband (and was a bit dramatic—hey, I own it) about how all I do is pour out, and then no one checks on me! Instead, everyone assumes I am fine. (See why I went to therapy?)

Of course, Seth responded time after time with how much I am loved and how if I *asked* for help, I would have a line of people ready to help. And that was the key. The people pleaser doesn't ask for help. We keep going until we collapse and sleep for days, get sick from depleting our physical reservoirs, or most commonly, have a meltdown. Or all three.

Why couldn't I see that in the moment? How was I getting caught in a chaos cycle? By believing thoughts that were not true. Sit in that previous sentence for a moment, don't rush through it.

My desire to keep my children and husband happy and satisfied, my family happy—even the happiness of strangers I might run into at the grocery store, ugh, we don't have time to get into that—was running me straight out of mental fuel. I had a depletion of willpower and broken boundaries, which then created a *yes* storm. A few *no's* were the better and healthier choice, but I failed to challenge my thought processes.

I don't know about you, but stress and anxiety are always there when my tank is depleted, and I get stuck. Like sidewalk gum lying out in the hot sun—not just sticky but stretchy too—they are just looking to hang on and make a mess everywhere we go.

A research study done by the American Psychological Association shows that willpower and self-control can be limited mental resources. So, if we use all our mental resources to make sure others have what they need and are taken care of, we have little to none left for ourselves. And in those moments, we are not able to say no.

Remember, the behavior is never the root; it is the symptom.

This is your space to map out what a cycle of chaos looks like for you.

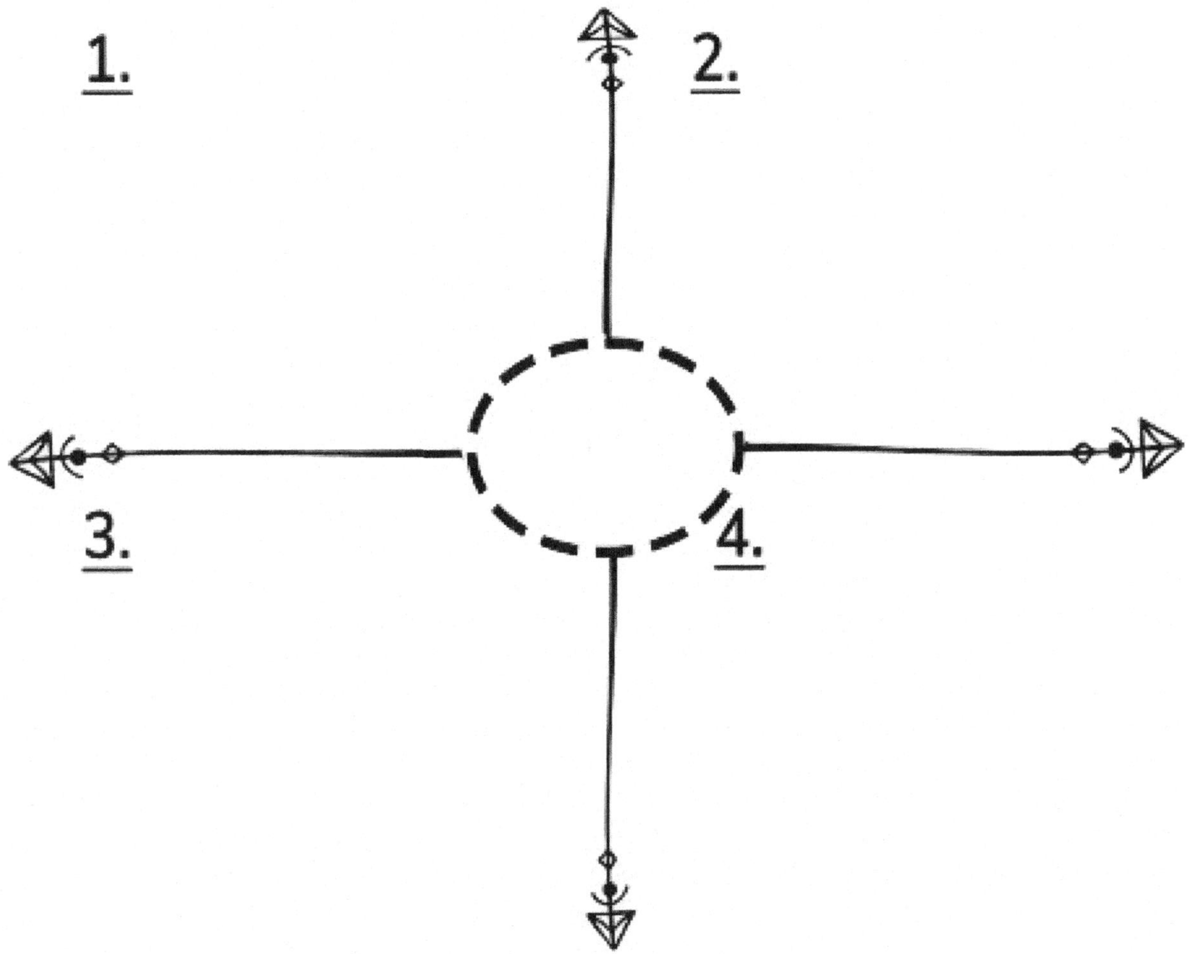

Phase Nine

The Eight Core Emotions

"Emotions are more effective when used to diagnose a problem than using them to repair one. Emotions are valid and useful. But how are you using your emotions? When used more like plumb lines and less like jackhammers, they esteem & honor relationships and self."

—Candace Payne

Core Emotions and Their Meaning

Think of your emotions as outerwear. Something that is visible to everyone and takes care of protecting you from the outside world. And think of it like the "brown ocean effect" I explained to you in the beginning of this book, specifically *your* "brown ocean effect."

In our past traumatic experiences, if we had no tools to break down the unhealthy cycles, it possibly resulted in destructive cycles in our lives, and we carried those patterns around via our feelings. And instead of seeing a circumstance as something new to be evaluated through the lens of a healthy heart and mind, an old unprocessed experience triggers an unhealthy response. And brings with it the potential to destroy things around you. Again. Make sense?

Phase Nine: The Eight Core Emotions

"All of our feelings are positive. All of them are good because all of them are important messengers."—Dr. Chip Dodd

The first time I read that statement by Dr. Chip Dodd, author of *The Voice of the Heart: A Call to Full Living*[22], I had the biggest ah-ha moment! Not just for myself personally, but for the clients that I counseled day in and day out.

I thought, "Do you mean to tell me anger is a good emotion? And what about grief, sadness, frustration, guilt, you know all those emotions we want to run, run, run far away from!

These emotions shame us and often find us embarrassed and apologizing for even having them in the first place—yeah, what about those, right? You mean to tell me, Dr. Dodd, those are good?"

I began to study this concept and think about anger, guilt, fear, and all kinds of other negative emotions as being effective and positive. I determined that they all do serve us in positive ways so let me break this down further and share with you the illustration I developed that helps me to teach my clients that all emotions are useful when controlled by the Spirit that gave them. And all emotions we experience apply to this concept.

For the sake of the book, I will focus on the primary eight core emotions we, as humans, experience. Not to say that these are the only emotions we have because as God knows if you are a woman, you probably have one

22 https://www.chipdodd.com/serviceslist *The Voice of the Heart: A Call to Full Living* Dodd, Chip, Sage Hill, LLC, 2015.

hundred nuances to each of these in just one day, right? I feel you friend—I am with you!

How can all emotions be good and serve as important messengers? Well, that's because emotions serve a **purpose**. Every last one does. God created us as emotional beings. He created us to feel and to experience connections all around us. It just comes down to what we do with our emotions. After all, **the root of emotion is motion, to move.** So, remember **an emotion has motion. Do we use our emotions to harm or to help?**

Every time I hear about any form of abuse, my flesh is beyond anger. But I can't use that anger in a negative way. Gossip, spreading slander, coming up with plans to harm that perpetrator, or putting a hit out for them (which seems like such a rational thought at the moment) is not how God's Word directs us. I have to channel that emotion for the good. I have to use that righteous anger and let it be my motivator for good.

So, how do I channel it? I stay involved with helping survivors of abuse. I counsel women and men who have gone through terrible forms of abuse. I pray for them, advocate for them, write curriculums that bring awareness and healing, and give away free classes for these survivors. These are productive ways to channel that anger.

We model and empower people to do the good with the emotion not the negative. The good is what produces more fruit.

The good is the key to finding your purpose, peace, and productivity.

For many, the mindset about emotions comes from a negative view. When it comes from a negative view one only sees it as just that—negative.

So, let's step back for a moment. Your Chapter One wasn't written by you, but before you were even born God knew you. He designed you in his image. You were not a mistake, mishap, or accident. You came into this world and had no baggage attached to you at birth. But SIN came in through those people in your first chapter—maybe your problems came because as a child you were around people living in sin, you were around abuse, or abuse happened to you, maybe you witnessed horrible violence, discriminations, drugs, divorce, or possibly you, yourself, made unhealthy choices in your teenage and early adult years.

Whatever the cause—you need to know that it is okay to have these emotions. If you are running from them, it's time to stop. It's time to face those feelings. You might be on the opposite end and feeling all the feelings and not know what to do with them. Together, we will face them, process them, and I will guide you to channel them in healthy ways.

So, let's look at some more examples of the eight common emotions. They are **sadness, anger, fear, hurt, loneliness, guilt, shame, and gladness.**

Sadness

The purpose of sadness is to teach us greater empathy.

In an ideal world, sadness is like an umbrella. We hold on to that umbrella when rainy days come, but we close that umbrella once we are in a safe and dry place. Sad things happen every day across the world. Just turn on the news or browse through social media, and you see sadness all around.

In difficult times, sadness serves a purpose, even if the traumatic event doesn't happen to us directly. **The purpose of sadness is to teach us greater empathy.**

Imagine a world with greater empathy. We certainly need it, and as we learn to give it we, in turn, receive it. I will go into greater detail on empathy because that is absolutely needed for us to write our second chapter, but I want to talk about when sadness doesn't serve a healthy purpose for this section.

I want to be clear that sadness and depression are not the same things. There is a major difference, and you must understand the difference. Sadness is a normal reaction after going through loss, disappointment, a difficult situation, an unexpected medical condition, or a significant life change.

Sadness comes and goes. Like an umbrella, we have rainy days and it's needed, and on other days, that umbrella is nowhere around. Sadness does typically go away on its own and usually won't impact your life significantly.

It's uncomfortable and doesn't feel good, but if it is true sadness, you can eventually get back to things that once brought you joy and purpose.

Though stuck for a time, you can move forward in a healthy, productive manner with the proper action steps. A good friend to remind you about your purpose and show empathy can go a long way for someone experiencing sadness. A kind word or prayer from a family member who has gone through a similar loss can boost someone experiencing sadness.

But, if we experience sadness (which I am sure we all have) and we don't grow from it, our hearts don't expand with more empathy, but instead, we grow frustrated, bitter, more controlling, then we are stuck. Stuck in a chaotic cycle of sadness means we are not learning.

Now, don't panic at this part. Instead, celebrate that you are reading this book, and will soon learn effective ways to get out of that chaos cycle.

Just like you would never question someone using an umbrella on a rainy day—if something sad happens in your life or around you—don't feel the need to justify or defend your sadness. Remember, this is a normal response. But if that sadness has been there for quite some time, maybe it's time to look a little deeper.

Depression isn't just sadness. Depression is a mental health illness and directly affects your moods, lasts longer than just two to three weeks, doesn't typically go away on its own, and greatly impacts your life. Depression affects the way you view and understand yourself.

When depressed, thoughts often center around worthlessness, hopelessness, and unreasonable amounts of guilt. During lows, depression makes us feel like we have no purpose, and we are probably better off not being on this earth. But I am here to tell you that is an absolute lie!

If depression is a current struggle, I recommend you find a therapist you trust and learn how to unpack these unhelpful thoughts. You don't need to continue this unhelpful cycle alone.

You are not the only one going through this; and remember, some people have spent many years in schooling and training to help people with depression. So take advantage of their knowledge and the tools they offer. It's their passion and privilege to walk alongside someone struggling. No one should have to die of depression. Ever.

This book, designed as a tool to assist your journey, is not a replacement for therapy and psychiatric services. Remember that.

When struggling with depression, I believe it is vital to use all the spiritual resources, psychological tools, and medical resources available. If someone has made you feel that you need to "pray away" your depression or possibly that you are not "spiritual" enough, and that is the reason for your depression—I am sorry. This is not true.

Sometimes we can do every spiritual thing we know to do, but yet it seems like not enough. For example, if your friend was diagnosed with diabetes and their doctor told them that they needed to take insulin every day—you would not tell them that they are not spiritual enough, and maybe that is why they have this diagnosis.

Yes, prayer works. Yes, God heals. But it is also our responsibility to do everything we can to take care of our bodies on earth, including our minds. Eating well, exercise, proper medications are all things we do if we have diabetes, right? But, for some reason, when it comes to mental health—especially when a Christian is struggling with depression—they often receive very hurtful comments about "how it's all in their mind" or "they are not spiritual enough." You know the words—the unhelpful and unsolicited advice. So yeah, tune that out.

Find a trusted group of professionals, spiritual leaders, and friends who will remind you how to get out of that mindset and extend empathy. And never forget your story because it will be your catalyst for writing your second chapter. From this struggle, empathy is born, and the same empathy that you often wished and prayed for others to give you, you will have to give freely. That, dear friends, is a gift that not all possess.

Anger

Just like sadness is a normal emotion from time to time, so is anger. At some time in your life, you have experienced anger—I often say I never considered myself a person to struggle with anger. But then I got married and lived with the same human day in and day out. Oh my goodness—now I know what anger feels like, and my typically funny jokester husband—also is very familiar with anger after being married to me for sixteen years. And this is why we have to keep talking to Jesus!

Think of anger as rain boots, footwear. Something that carries us through dirty places, even places with hidden hazards like broken glass or unseen rocks that can tear at our feet. Our feet move us from place to place and need protection from things that hinder our stride.

Anger is never the root of any behavior. Anger is a protective mechanism against a perceived threat. Anger signals a crossed boundary.

Many see anger as a negative, destructive emotion, but it's not. Only unchecked anger and rage are destructive. That uncontrolled anger is dangerous and does not serve a useful purpose whatsoever. It is also sinful. Unhealthy anger hurt others. It's a destructive catalyst for selfish or prideful retaliatory actions and has no rational thoughts and actions.

If you or someone you know falls into unhealthy anger, then they need to seek help. Accommodating an angry person's violence or allowing them to control us because we fear they will "explode in anger" or become violent with rage never teaches them to master their anger. Instead, it merely feeds it and makes the problem worse in the end because we are "pacifying," also known as enabling them to continue exercising total control using their rage. It's teaching them nothing effective that can be used in the future and only reinforces that when they get angry and explode, they get their way.

Anger's purpose is to teach us greater self-control.

Sounds like a spoiled child throwing a tantrum and the parents giving in to them, so they stop crying, right? Pacifying a child's temper tantrum produces a momentary reprieve for the parent while reinforcing bad behavior in the child. What do you think the child will continue to do in the future when he isn't getting his way? Same with an adult, except you have adult-size displays of strength that can injure and kill.

Anger, when harnessed, is a tool—a tool for action. **Anger's purpose is to teach us greater self-control.** Remember, rain or work boots are great for serving the purpose of messy, wet jobs but ruin light-colored carpeted floors.

Fear

Fear is like our eye covering, our sunglasses. They block the blinding sunlight. In the same way I have explained that sadness and anger are normal responses and if handled an effective manner they can be great teachers, well, so is fear. Everyone should have a healthy amount of fear. Like I tell my clients who come into my office for therapy due to high levels of fear and anxiety. No fear is not healthy and having too much fear isn't healthy either. Healthy fear is what gets us up in the morning, it's a motivator for completing work tasks or responsibilities, it's what keeps us on a search to find and know our creator and it is what will make me pack my bags and leave south Louisiana next time a strong hurricane is brewing in the Gulf of Mexico.

Fear's purpose is to teach us faith with action.

But sometimes, fear doesn't stop at the healthy level. Fear, when unchecked, wreaks havoc on the mind any and every chance it gets, attempting to block all rational thoughts. Fear covers our minds. Instead of helping us see clearer, it blinds us and causes us to lose track of our faith. It blocks us from the son, Jesus. How?

Well, we become more focused on wondering (the speculation kind, not the awe-inspiring kind), worry, and doubt than on the peace, love, and joy that comes from knowing and focusing on the truth of God's Word. Speculation takes the place of knowledge, and imagination supersedes the truth. As a result, we lose the clarity needed for appropriate reactions and to make good decisions.

Fear's purpose is to teach us faith with action. When we are struggling with fear, we are really struggling with faith that is stuck. And sometimes not even just faith in God, but more, so faith in ourselves to be an overcomer. By ourselves we can't be overcomers, but with God, we are more than conquerors.

Hurt

Gloves are the covering that envelopes hands and hides what's beneath. A glove hides the condition of the hands. Once gloved, except for size, all hands look the same. Such it is so with hurt: we may look just like every other fully functioning adult on the outside, but we are hiding a lifetime of pain behind that gracious, happy facade.

The saying that people who are hurting hurt other people is not off the mark. You may not think this is so, but believe me when I tell you that though it may not have happened yet, you will crash and burn. You see, hurt does not lie dormant. It builds. And it takes on another name. Bitterness.

Bitterness comes out in subtle and not-so-subtle ways. It's evident in the woman who treats her husband as though he were the one who abused her, making him pay for the sins of the man who did. It rears its resentful head when it displays its offense at every slight, whether real or imagined.

Since bitterness cannot abide with joy, it finds no pleasure in anything and tends to withhold things from others so that they are miserable too. Is this looking more familiar? Is hurt normal? Yup. It sure is. We live in a fallen, sinful world where people do unrighteous things that cause great pain to someone else. So yes, hurt is a real emotional wound that does need doctoring. And Jesus is the greatest physician for that hurt. **Hurt's purpose is to teach you forgiveness.**

Loneliness

Loneliness serves the purpose of teaching us the importance of connection.

Loneliness is like a poncho. It is all-engulfing and covers like a web making one feel like one can't break free. Loneliness isolates and gives the impression that we are "fighting this battle alone."

In the book of 1 Kings, chapter 19, Elijah the prophet has a moment where he feels forsaken. God asks Elijah what he's doing in that cave. As though God didn't already know the answer. Nevertheless, Elijah replies, *"I am the only one left, and now they are trying to kill me, too."*

There is a difference between loneliness and aloneness. God will separate us from others to get us alone with him so he can speak to us. What is God's response to Elijah? We find it in Romans as the writer retells the story.

God responded, *"I have reserved for Myself seven thousand men who have not bowed the knee to Baal."* That's the equivalent of God saying, "Don't worry. I've got you right where I want you for the purpose I have already planned."

Just as God's presence and assurance to Elijah were not in the violence of a storm but a still, small voice, when we allow God to enter our circumstances and talk over the situations with him, he will speak to us.

For so long, I stayed busy running from stillness. I was afraid of the silence and my racing thoughts. Is this you too?

I began the healing process by joining my heavenly Father to face the past and all its chaos and hurt. Then, the stillness became a friend. The quiet is now a salve, promoting healing to those wounds that left me hurting and feeling lonely. **Loneliness serves the purpose of teaching us the importance of connection.**

Guilt

Guilt is like a hat, except it does more than cover our heads. It covers our minds, thought processes, and our ability to make decisions with clarity and motives, not tinged with the need to "make amends" for things we own that are not our faults.

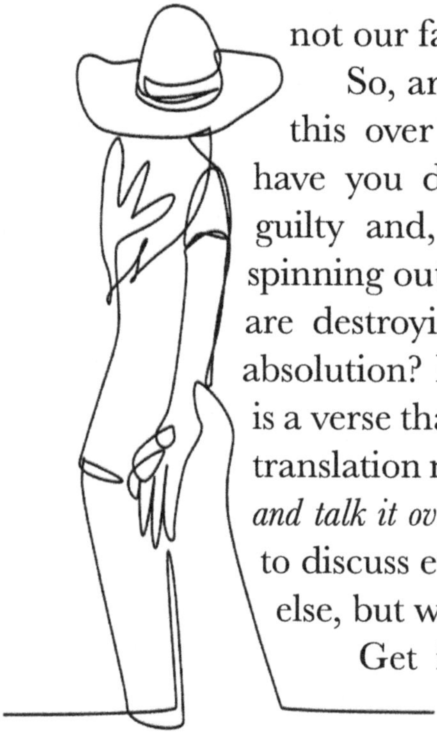

So, are you talking all this over with God? Or have you decided you are guilty and, like a cyclone spinning out of control, you are destroying yourself with your attempts to gain absolution? In the book of Isaiah, chapter one, there is a verse that starts with *"let us reason together."* Another translation makes it clearer: *"I, the Lord, invite you to come and talk it over."* Okay, it seems to me that God wants to discuss every part of your life, not with everybody else, but with you. What to do?

Guilt serves to teach us peace.

Get in conversation with God and ask him the reason for the guilt? Is it useful? Is it yours to own? Here's the thing about God, he will not make you repay a debt you don't owe. Calvary proved that.

Furthermore, the devil is your accuser, not God. (Revelation 12:10) There is a difference between condemnation and conviction. Condemnation causes us to run from God. Conviction draws us to the One that sent it. **Guilt serves to teach us peace.**

Shame

Shame is like a trench coat; it is all covering and holds separates. Shame tells us we will never have a blessed life because of what we have done. It says everyone knows what we have done, and we are hypocritical to attend church, read our Bibles, and change our lifestyles.

It says past sexual abuse means we have to allow others to misuse us sexually. After all, we are damaged goods. We see ourselves as in control if we are the ones that give "consent" to the sex. Shame says stay silent. We can't come out from that covering that's protecting us from exposure to the harshness of reality.

Shame serves the purpose of teaching us honor and respect.

But are we protecting ourselves, or are we suffering in silence? Do our pasts make us hypocrites when we change, or do our histories make us wiser and able to become teachers of the better way we have found?

The Bible recounts the story of Elkanah and his two wives, Peninnah and Hannah. In biblical times, barrenness was a shameful condition. Though Peninnah gave her husband a child, Hannah had failed to conceive, and Peninnah provoked and taunted her concerning her failure to conceive a child. As a result, Hannah felt shame at her condition.

> *"The Lord brings death and makes alive; he brings down to the grave and raises up. The Lord sends poverty and wealth; he humbles, and he exalts. He raises the poor from the dust and lifts the needy from the ash heap; he seats them with princes and has them inherit a throne of honor"* (1 Samuel 2:6–8 NIV).

Let me remind you that God is the redeemer of our condition. He is the one that gives us our identity and purpose. Failures become part of the story of our successes.

Gladness

The purpose of gladness is sharing and generosity.

Gladness is our bag of good things and the lining of that bag is gratitude. Gratitude is the state of being grateful and is possibly one of the most undervalued tools for balancing emotions and keeping us appreciating all the positive parts of our lives. **The purpose of gladness is sharing and generosity.**

> *"Worship the Lord with gladness; come before him with joyful songs."*
>
> (Psalm 100:2)

Phase Ten

Unhealthy Core Beliefs

"You can never learn that Christ is all you need, until Christ is all you have." — Corrie Ten Boom

Do you need further convincing as to why confronting abuse or abandonment experiences is important? Sometimes friends, family members, or even a Christian counselor may say, "That was so long ago. It's in the past. Just forgive, get over it, and get on with your life."

Maybe you've given that message to yourself. After all, you survived, didn't you? You understand now what happened to you. So, what more do you need to do? The answer lies in recognizing some of the deeper layers of trauma.

Until we get specific about what has wounded us, we won't know where the healing needs to happen or what action is needed for the healing to stick.

Trauma profoundly affects our thinking and how we cope. Our experiences in our families of origin, especially our trauma experiences, have programmed our thinking patterns and behaviors. To break those unhealthy patterns, we have to first identify what they are. Until we get specific about what has wounded us, we won't know where the healing needs to happen or what action is needed for the healing to stick.

Core Beliefs That Alter the Mind:

I am a bad or unworthy person.

This unhealthy or faulty core belief is due to shame. Shame is the belief that *I am someone bad,* rather than that *I have done something bad.* Our feelings about our behavior are called guilt. Our negative feelings about ourselves are called shame. Stay here a little while and think through the difference between guilt and shame.

Unhealthy family dynamics such as *family silence*, the "no talk" rule, may add to our shame. We may have never had a safe place to share our feelings and experiences, so we absorb the bad experience with its guilt and inner conflict and the shame that comes with all of it.

Guilt is about performance; shame is about personhood, i.e., how we feel about ourselves.

A perpetrator often tells a child the abuse is her fault. It's one way of ensuring the victim's silence. When victims are blamed for their trauma, they internalize the belief: "I must be a terrible person."

If we believe we are bad, worthless, and horrible, we won't think we deserve to receive healing and peace. We won't pursue it. We may not even let others help us.

No one would love me as I am.

Trauma creates a shameful sense of being defective. It also spawns the false belief that we are unlovable.

As an adult, we know the ways we've coped with the trauma of our childhoods and teen years. We know the substances and behaviors we've used to medicate our pain or to find some morsel of affirmation.

Consequently, we'll guard our hidden parts carefully. It's too dangerous to let the secrets out. We'll avoid, manipulate, and even lie to keep from being discovered. The risk of further abandonment is simply too great.

No one will meet my needs.

If as a child our most basic needs for time, attention, affection, and nurture aren't met—not to mention our physical needs for survival and safety—we fail to develop a sense that the world is a safe place. If there's no hope for getting our needs met, then why ask? What's the point?

Because of the "don't talk" and "don't feel" rules of our families, we usually learn, at an early age, to keep our needs to ourselves.

Sex is my most important need.

Relationships are not optional. God created us for human connection. He made us relational beings, intended for intimacy with other human beings as well as with him.

Our need for connection through relationships is our most basic nonphysical need. It's our core longing.

When this legitimate need isn't met by our earthly parents, it's exacerbated. It grows deeper. It becomes painful. Because of the tragedy of the sexual abuse most of us have experienced, this God-given need for a relationship is often perverted into a need for sex.

> *"Do not conform any longer to the pattern of this world but be transformed by the renewing of your mind. Then you will be able to test and approve what God's will is—his good, pleasing and perfect will"* (Romans 12:2).

> *"You intended to harm me, but God intended it for good to accomplish what is now being done, the saving of many lives"* (Genesis 50:20).

What are your unhealthy core beliefs? Ask Jesus for his help in identifying them. Jesus is the foundation that will never crumble beneath the weight of your past. Let him help you.

Phase Eleven

The Family Rules

"You're disturbed by the very thought of expressing anything negative about your parents. The old tape that commands, 'Honor thy father and thy mother' is playing loudly in your ear.

There is no dishonor in telling the truth. It is always honorable to state the truth. It's important to remember that understanding is different from blaming. When we understand our baggage, we can stop being burdened by it."

—Marnie C. Ferree (No Stones)

"*.... the truth will set you free" (*John 8:32).

The enemy is a liar, and he wants you to believe you can't talk about your family at this moment. The truth is the truth and what you don't reveal, can't be healed! Your experiences of childhood and your upbringing have shaped the wounds of today.

It is important to understand, there is no perfect family, and we must accept that. No father or mother will ever be perfect, and only one Father can claim the title of perfect Father and that is Christ Jesus.

God's design for the family was perfect, but sin entered the world through Adam and Eve and the family relationship forever changed after that. All of us have been born into a family marked by sin and imperfection. All of us are replicating those problems in our own families, at least to some extent.

Unhealthy Families and the Rules That Rule

These are the unspoken rules in families which provide no health to a family system.

1. **Don't talk:** The "don't talk" rule is common in many family homes. This is the family who talks but doesn't talk about the important things like the family secrets, the family problems, the difficult emotions, and the mistakes parents made along the way. To the outsider it may appear this family are close and communicate, but when in reality they dodge all hard conversations. This can leave members of the family feeling unheard and undervalued. It is also a breeding ground in which healthy trust is not shown because truth isn't spoken.

2. **Don't feel:** The "don't feel" rule in the family means we stay away from the hard emotions such as sadness, anger, frustration, rage, confusion, loneliness, but are free to feel happiness and joy. Avoiding expressions of emotion can cause emotional numbness, spiritual sleeping, depression, shutdowns, and explosions of rage. It often leaves family members feeling like they are not allowed to have emotions and if they do are made to feel that the emotion displayed is not accepted or validated.

3. **Deny or minimize:** When a family doesn't talk and doesn't feel, it usually substitutes alternate ways of coping with life: denial and blame. Have you ever tried to tell a parent how you feel or how you are unable to express yourself and then suddenly you are the problem? You are the one to blame. Or worse, it is denied altogether and minimized as though you are making a bigger deal about it than is warranted.

4. **Other unhealthy family rules:** (Keep in mind these family rules are often unspoken, but you recognize this is a family rule by the way your parents or caregivers behaved.)

    - Dad (or Mom) is always right.
    - Don't upset Mom (or Dad).
    - Children are to be seen and not heard.
    - It's your job to take care of everyone else.
    - Boys are more valued than girls and get the best of everything.
    - Our religious views are always right and are not to be questioned.
    - Appearances are crucial; what people think of us governs how we behave.
    - A woman is nothing without a man.
    - Financial success is the measure of human worth.
    - Making a mistake is the worst thing you can do.

What unspoken or spoken rules were front and center in your home growing up? Do any of the above resonate with you?

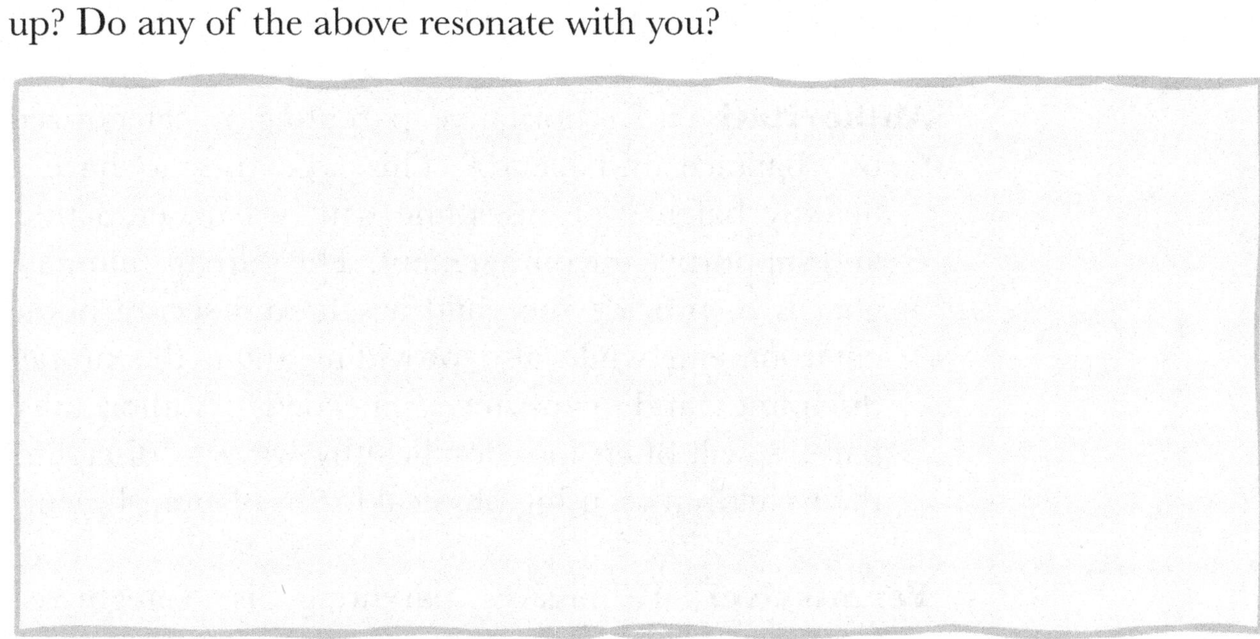

Parenting Styles

While taking a deeper dive into unhealthy family rules, I want you to also take a look at what type of parenting style you grew up under. This is simply a quick description of the most common parenting styles, but if you are interested in this section and diving a bit deeper, definitely take some time to do some reading on parenting styles. You can find a wealth of information on parenting styles online.

Authoritarian: Authoritarian parenting is categorized by a strict discipline style. These parents are not flexible and give very little grace and mercy toward the children. The parents' ultimate goal is obedience from the child, and they do not want to be questioned by the child. They believe in the motto of "do as I say and without question." This parenting style can use physical punishments, such as spanking, slapping, or having the child kneel for long periods of time.

Authoritative: Authoritative parenting is categorized by "balance and blend." This type tries to have a healthy balance of discipline with warm, empathic, and supportive encouragement. The parents' ultimate goal is to provide the child a safe and secure home environment, while also providing them the proper discipline and consistency needed. Authoritative parents will often look for healthy ways to discipline their children vs. using physical forms of punishment.

Permissive: Permissive parenting is categorized by warm, loving, nurturing parenting, but also inconsistency in discipline. These parents typically will not require their children to have chores or major responsibilities. The children's days are typically not very structured. Permissive parents have a hard time telling their children no and as a result the children don't learn that no is an option and life doesn't revolve around the wants of the child.

Uninvolved: Uninvolved parenting is truly sad because the parents do not meet their child's emotional or physical needs or sometimes both. The parents are just not involved with their children and provide very little supervision. They are the opposite of the "helicopter" parent. They are uninvolved because they give their attention to something "more pressing"—whether it's their job, ministry work, an unhealthy needy relationship, drug addiction, or mental health issues—whatever the reason the fact remains, their children are not a top priority.

What Are Generational Sins?

"Our ancestors sinned and are no more, and we bear their punishment" (Lamentations 5:7).

"Search me, God, and know my heart; test me and know my anxious thoughts. See if there is any offensive way in me and lead me in the way everlasting" (Psalm 139: 23–24).

"However, if you do not obey the Lord your God and do not carefully follow all his commands and decrees, I am giving you today, all these curses will come on you and overtake you" (Deuteronomy 28:15).

It doesn't take much digging into our family systems to see how patterns of thoughts, behaviors, and feelings repeat themselves in families. Many of us may think of the common addictions, such as drugs and alcohol, and easily see how they are repeated from generation to generation in some families. Generational sins can be defined as sinful weaknesses or tendencies passed down through the generations of a family. They involve behavioral patterns or ways of thinking and feeling.

A biblical example of a generational sin was one started by Abram lying about his relationship with his wife, Sarai.

He told Sarai to tell people she was his sister instead of his wife. Abram feared the Egyptians would kill him and take his wife.

Fast-forward to Isaac and a continuation of this lying spirit. Same situation. Isaac told the men of Gerar that his wife, Rebekah, was his sister. Same reason. Rebekah was beautiful and Isaac feared the men of Gerar would kill him and take Rebekah.

When fear and doubt presented themselves using the same threat, both father and son lied instead of trusting God.

Here are some examples of sins that can be found from generation to generation:

- Possessiveness (greed, jealousy, laziness, gambling, stealing).
- Sexual Sins (lust, fornication, adultery, pornography, incest, rape, sexual abuse of others).
- Anger Issues (unforgiveness, bitterness, hatred, rage, violence, aggressiveness toward others, revenge, murder).
- Substance Addictions (illegal drugs, abuse of prescription medication, alcohol, tobacco, food).
- Rebellion (stubbornness, pride, idolatry, disobedience, lawlessness, witchcraft, arrogance).

- ❖ Covenant Breaking (adultery, broken agreements or contracts, not keeping promises).
- ❖ False Religions / Occult Involvement (witchcraft, satanism, religious cults, voodoo, legalism).
- ❖ Critical Spirit (critical evaluation of others, judgmentalism, belittling others, self-righteousness, rejection of others, gossip).
- ❖ Uncontrolled Tongue (lying, slander, cursing, swearing, exaggeration, denial, gossip).

What Are Generational Curses?

Curses are spoken words. There is power in words. Proverbs tells us that the power of life and death are in our words. God created this world by speaking it into existence. When Jesus was on earth, he was in a boat during a storm, and he said, "Peace, be still," and stopped the storm with his words.

My friend Viviane tells how a friend of hers once spoke something very fear filled and negative about a circumstance in Viviane's life. My friend said she walked away from that conversation, talking to Jesus, saying, "Lord, I refuse that curse. In Jesus' name." Viviane said to me, "No one is allowed to speak that kind of negativity into my life."

I say yes! We all need to be like Viviane. Life and death are indeed in the power of our words. Instead of absorbing the negative projections people ignorantly and innocently speak, we need to refuse those words.

In the New Testament, James writes about curses in James chapter three. And throughout the Scriptures, Jesus speaks concerning the power of words again and again. In another place in Proverbs, chapter 26, it tells us that just like a bird that flutters about with no place to land, so it is with a curse.

A curse cannot have an impact if there's no place to land. So, you ask yourself, is there anything in my life that provides a place for a curse to land and take root? Am I allowing the careless negative words of others or myself to land when I should be refusing those words?

A generational curse can sound like:

- You can't do anything right.
- You are beyond help.
- You are stupid.
- You are ugly.
- You never listen.
- You will never learn.

You can also curse yourself with negative self-talk whether spoken out loud or inwardly. This is extremely damaging to the human psyche and does not please the God who created us. Remember, he created us in his image so when we speak these things we are saying them about the original as well.

Regardless of if we heard this spoken to us our entire lives or we spoke this about ourselves in the past, we can end it now and not allow it to be spoken by us about ourselves or to the generations that come after us.

What Are Soul Ties?

A spiritual or emotional connection we have to someone after being sexually intimate with them or through a cultlike emotional connection to a personality is a soul tie. It's as though they possess an intangible part of us and hold a connectedness to us though we may no longer be in a relationship with them.

Unhealthy soul ties develop through sin. One example is sexual sin. The Scripture teaches that through sexual intimacy, two distinct persons become one. We understand that people don't physically become one. It's the souls that unite and become "tied." (Genesis 2:24) The Hebrew understanding of becoming one flesh goes far beyond the physical joining of two bodies; there's a joining of the essence of their beings.

The apostle Paul, in 1 Corinthians, chapter 6, commands that a man should not join with a prostitute because, in that merging, the two become one. Paul warns against sexual activity that would create a soul tie between two people who engage in sex without marital commitment.

A second example is soul ties that develop through misplaced trust, fear, and the need for approval, i.e., the fear of man. Again, this is in relationships of an emotional or spiritual nature, where people have entrusted themselves to other individuals in an almost cultic environment.

There's something that happens in these spiritual oaths and prayers. A spiritual connection is made that creates an unhealthy influence on people's lives. It opens the possibility for manipulation by the opinions, the resources, and the pleasures of other people. We are controlled instead of living in freedom when this occurs, and a soul tie is an outcome.

When we are more dependent upon or fearful of or influenced by what someone else thinks about us than what God thinks and what God says, that is an unhealthy soul tie that needs destroying.

Third, soul ties result from abuse and violation. Sexual violation and abuse cause more than just humiliation and indignity. A perverted connection takes place as the victim experiences horrible manipulation. The abused one feels a lot of guilt and betrayal. They may find it hard to break loose from the person using them. These abuses and violations can affect the mind and emotions. And they can affect the will of the victim. So there needs to be a severing of that soul tie.

Finally, soul ties do not cultivate a person's improvement; instead, they foster control, manipulation, self-interest, and shame. Biblically unhealthy relationships bring about the debilitating strongholds of confusion and anxiety, unrest, shame, guilt, and oppression. All these things come out of soul ties.

This evaluation is a heavy one, but it doesn't have to be a fearful one. Ask God to be with you and help you look at this to identify it, challenging the patterns and breaking free of them for your lifetime and that of the generations to come behind you. It is a legacy of freedom.

A useful prayer: *Dear God, I pray that you show me the generational sin, curses, and soul ties in my life and their roots and set me free from these in Jesus' name.*

Dismantling Generational Sins, Generational Curses, and Soul Ties

Leviticus 26:40–42 is a prescription that God gives the nation of Israel concerning how to break generational sins and curses: *"But if they confess their iniquity and the iniquity of their fathers in their treachery that they committed against me, and also in walking contrary to me…then I will remember my covenant with Jacob, and I will remember my covenant with Isaac and my covenant with Abraham, and I will remember the land."*

How do we dismantle generational issues once we've identified them? We use the 4 *R's*—**R**epentance, **R**ebuke, **R**eplace, **R**eceive.

1.Repentance

Repentance in Scripture means an about-face (to turn around and go in a different direction). It's to feel regret or contrition, to turn from sin and dedicate yourself to changing your behaviors. So likewise, dismantling generational issues requires an about-face, refusing to allow that sin to remain active in our lives. So we repent for ourselves and our past family legacy. This action on our part means we begin a future legacy that is different from the one to which we were born.

2.Rebuke

While repentance turns something away, rebuking keeps it away. We can turn away, but it's in the rebuking, the binding, the tying up of that thing that stops it. We are given that power by the Holy Spirit that lives in us.

> *"Truly I tell you, whatever you bind on earth will be bound in heaven, and whatever you loose on earth will be loosed in heaven"* (Matthew 18:18).

3.Replace

Replacing is just what it sounds like, once we have repented of something and rebuked it, there is an empty space where something wholesome and healthy can live.

Where I once had a mouth filled with profanity, I now have a mouth filled with praise to God. Where I once turned to alcohol to numb and hide from my problems, I now turn to God in prayer and read my Bible to find the healing words written there.This replacement happens in all areas, little by little. But it has to happen. Remember me sharing in Chapter Two, Phase Three about doing the hard things? Yeah, this is it for you too. But good news, I have no superpower of my own. And the same God that draws you near him will give you the power to make those replacements the same as he did for me.

Allow God to lead you into righteousness. Making different decisions produces different results. God calls us to the uncomfortable to bring us to a new level of comfort.

4.Receive

Psalm 84, verse 6 talks about righteous people, those made right with God and by God, pass through the Valley of Baca. The word Baca means weeping.

This Scripture confirms that in the process of healing, there is weeping. But look at the next verse. It says, *"They go from strength to strength, till each appears before God in Zion."* Instead of looking at this as a harmful loss, view it as a healthy one. You are losing the things that have kept you trapped for too long.

Now receive with gratitude the thing that God has helped you to gain. You may not see it yet in the physical but with your heart and mind thank him as though you are already seeing it.

> *"Now faith is confidence in what we hope for and assurance about what we do not see"* (Hebrews 11:1).

By acknowledging with thanksgiving that God has helped you, you have entered into "now faith."

Here is an example of the 4 R's in place (I use the sin of lying).

Dear Lord, I come to you and humbly repent for a lying tongue. I repent of these sins and the sins of my family's generational patterns of lying.

I rebuke a lying spirit in the name of Jesus and I replace a lying tongue with a tongue that only speaks truth. A tongue that only honors you. God, I give you all the glory and the honor and I receive the freedom that is available to me through the power of the Holy Spirit. In Jesus' name. Amen.

Another example using the 4 R's to pray for the breakage of a soul tie.

Dear Lord, I humbly come to you repenting of my past sexual sin where I developed unhealthy soul ties.

In the name of Jesus, I rebuke the power and control this soul tie had over me physically, mentally, and spiritually. Lord, please sever this soul tie once and for all.

Give me the strength to enforce healthy boundaries that are pleasing to you. I replace all unhealthy boundaries with righteous behaviors that honor you.

God, I give you all the glory and the honor and I receive the freedom that is available to me through the power of the Holy Spirit. In Jesus' name. Amen.

Let's look at an example dealing with generational curses and how you can use the 4 R's.

The curse: "You can't do anything right!"

The replacement response: "I can do all things through Christ which strengthens me." Therefore, I declare that I can do anything that is in the will of God. Thank you, Lord Jesus, for the power of your Word and the ability to replace and receive the freedom you have available for me.

One other note here: when things go wrong, or you make a mistake, do you say something like "I'm so stupid"? If so, stop it. You are not stupid.

The choice may not have been wise, but a better response is, "Lord, I made an unwise choice. Please forgive me. You made me smarter than that choice. Teach me to make better choices and to recognize a trap before I get caught in it."

See the difference? We are acknowledging God's design, a.k.a. us, is a smart design. God is willing and able to teach us to be better and to do better.

It is our responsibility to trust him to do just that and to give us the power to learn a better way and live a better life.

Your Second Chapter

1. Do a personal inventory of generational sins, curses, and soul ties.

2. Practice the 4 R's and pray.

The book of Psalms already has wonderful prayer examples for us to use. When reading the Psalms, I encourage you to personalize the prayers written there.

Look at Psalm 79:8–9. Making a passage of Scripture a personal prayer can look something like this:

"Dear Jesus, Do not hold against me and my children the ______________ (whatever it is: lying, stealing, drug use, porn, adultery) of my family; may your mercy come quickly to meet us, for we are in desperate need.

Help us, God our Savior, for the glory of your name; deliver us and forgive our sins for your name's sake. In Jesus' name I pray. Amen." (Compare the sample prayer to the Scripture. Search the Psalms and you will find prayers for all the battles you face.) Then comes that gratitude, thanksgiving, praise, and worship.

Chapter Two

Walking Into Peace, Purpose, & Productivity

No one gets to write the first chapter of their lives.

But everyone gets to write their second chapter.

At what point are you going to move from victim to overcomer?

From Chapter One to Chapter Two.

The choice is fully yours to make.

It's your time to write your next chapter.

Give yourself permission to step into your Chapter Two.

No more being stuck.

Phase One

Making Room

"If we want to make room for Chapter Two, we have to first stop trying to be the boss!"
— Vera

Now that you have learned why we can stay stuck, it's time to move into the action steps. It's time to get out of the mud, step by step.

The first step in getting out of the cycle of chaos is taking a look at your thoughts. If your mindset is still coming up with many reasons why you can't move, that is the place you start. After that, it is time to make room for *your* Chapter Two.

Over the years, whether it was my early struggles with abandonment, hurt from family relationships, people-pleasing problems, marriage problems, the beast of depression, or the unrested mind of anxiety, I would find myself praying and begging God to "change those situations!" I repeatedly asked God to change the situation because that was the easiest way I knew to get immediate relief. It was much easier to look at others who contributed to the problem because, to my way of thinking, they caused this in the first place.

My anguished cries of, "Lord, just change this situation! Change my husband! Heal my body! Fix this financial situation we are in!" seemed to go unheard or unanswered. Ugh. Don't you love how bossy I can be with God? I mean, who did I think I was? Like God is one to be bossed around.

Ever remember seeing that Esurance commercial where Beatrice doesn't understand how Facebook works?

Her friend tells her, "That's not how any of this works." Yeah, I was Beatrice, and God was the friend saying, "That's not how any of this works, Vera." It does make one want to say, "I unfriend you.", except it's God, and deep down, we know he exactly knows how everything works. Ever so patiently, God gently taught me. How? By not immediately answering my bossy request. The Lord would drop in my spirit:

"Vera, pray for me to change you!"

Wait…come again, Lord?

crickets

(bossy request, a.k.a "prayer request," again)

"Vera, pray for me to change you."

Waittttt…That's not God's voice. Satan's trying to discourage me.

And so, it continued, like a bad movie script, The Know-It-All versus The Creator of the Universe. Finally, I'm getting a clue. An unwanted one.

Wait…you mean I need to change?!

Oh, I asked God the same question in a bunch of different ways. You know how we do. Oh, it's only me that does that? Yeah, that's what I thought. Anyway, while you're in denial, I'll continue truthing.

God, you're going to have to clarify that.

But I think I have already changed a lot…like really a lot!"

sniff

- It was painful.

Okay, I know. That wasn't a very humble response. The Lord asks a question. (Don't you want just to pretend you didn't hear the ask? Again, just me?)

"Do you think you ever get to a place where you stop spiritually maturing?"

God, why are you always showing me ways to be humble?

I am hurting here!

I am broken.

I really don't want any more lessons.

Can you see why God has had a time with me? The questions! I always want to know why. And then I was looking for quick ways to escape the pain. Just take it away. No more lessons here, God.

And guess what, the majority of the time, I never found out why. And then, sometimes, after I learned the lesson and humbled myself, and I submitted myself earnestly to seeking God, which enabled me to do that really hard thing, the answer to the *why* came.

The answer to *why* doesn't always come first or second or even in the middle of the pain—the answer comes after we take the leap of faith and become obedient to dealing with the pain God's way. He is looking for us to ask *what*, not *why*. What would you have me do with this, Lord?

I have a friend who says, "I'd much rather have a bone-deep assurance from God than an explanation." Hum, seems like I've read that somewhere.

> *"Now faith is confidence in what we hope for and assurance about what we do not see"* (Hebrews 11:1).

With assurance comes the patience to wait on an explanation that we may not get until heaven. And knowing why doesn't change what happened or make it any easier to accept. We ask *why*, as though God needs our approval on what he allowed to happen. Nada.

So, there I was, at a crossroads with my bossy request to God. I had to decide to stay stuck in my pain or allow God to change me. After all, the only one I had control over was me. I couldn't change my parents. I couldn't change my husband, and I certainly couldn't change all the God-ordained events happening around me.

So, finally, I submitted my bossy, independent self to God's request. And it wasn't after the first time he dropped his will into my spirit. It was after many, many years of my staying in the cycle of chaos. Read that again—many, many, YEARS.

You would think I would have gotten tired of being in the cycle of chaos that lived in my mind, but you know some people are more stubborn than others. Obviously, I fall into that more stubborn category. And wow, it's crowded there.

I finally got the memo and started changing my script. The new script became, "Jesus change me!" Not, "Oh Jesus, change every single person around me so that my life can be more peaceful!" When I prayed, "Jesus change me," he started to replace the overwhelmed mindset I was living with into one of God-given peace.

The mindset of "I can't do this anymore" became "God, provide me the strength to endure hard things." Day by day, God began to give me everything I needed to weather the storms that came my way.

Instead of praying for storms to never come, I gave up trying to control what was never in my power. I started writing a new script for my life. The words were ones of absolute faith that God keeps his word to me where he promised in Scripture never to leave me or forsake me. (Deuteronomy 31:6)

"Oh God, thank you for giving me everything I need to weather this storm. I trust you will do that for me, and you will do that for my family. You are the almighty comforter and I thank you for what will be done!"

New script! New script!

Your turn. Take some time and practice writing out a new script over a situation that has been plaguing you recently.

Phase Two

Renewing Your Mind

"Changing how you think changes how you live."
— Vera

The Importance of a Renewed Mind

I want to start this out by saying that the insecure attachments discussed over in Chapter One don't have to stay for the remainder of our lives. There is hope in Jesus and I want you to know that God hardwired our brains for change. Let me explain.

Romans 12:2 tells us that though our spirits are born again, our minds are not. Our minds, instead, must be renewed.

> *"Don't copy the behavior and customs of this world, but let God transform you into a new person by changing the way you think. Then you will learn to know God's will for you, which is good and pleasing and perfect"* (NLT).

God transforms us by changing the way we process thoughts, feelings, and circumstances. Need some proof from science? Okay. American psychologist Adam Grant discusses in his book *Think Again* how we frequently change our tastes in fashion or entertainment but are reluctant to change our way of thinking and emotional processing. He writes:

> *"Psychologists call it seizing and freezing: We favor the comfort of conviction over the discomfort of doubt, and we let our beliefs get brittle long before our bones. We laugh at people who still use Windows 95, yet we cling to opinions that we formed in 1995. We listen to views that make us feel good, instead of ideas that make us think hard."*

And this is what he says about the ability to change our thinking:

> *"Intelligence is traditionally viewed as the ability to think and learn. Yet in a turbulent world, there's another set of cognitive skills that might matter more: the ability to rethink and unlearn."*

What does the beginning of Isaiah 1:18 say? It says, *"'Come now, and let us reason together,' saith the Lord"* (KJV). This is God saying, 'Let's discuss this, you and me." Created and Creator. He's wanting to change our minds. Settle us into his way of thinking about our sin. Guess what? He has an opinion about everything that concerns us. And he gave us the ability to renew, that is restore, make new again, our minds.

Therefore, it's of utmost importance that you take on the work of changing the way you think. How do you do that? You challenge your thoughts.

Why do you want to do that? Well, you and I are *"fearfully and wonderfully made"* according to Psalm 139:14. And God has given us direction for this in Philippians 4:8:

"Finally, brothers and sisters, whatever is true, whatever is noble, whatever is right, whatever is pure, whatever is lovely, whatever is admirable—if anything is excellent or praiseworthy—think about such things."

Notice how it kind of reads like a command: Think like this! God knew we would struggle with our minds which in turn would affect our faith.

Our heads house a computer known as our brains. The housing is also host to our minds. This next little bit is a small lesson about the mind but bear with me and read it through. It will help you understand why it's so important to take your thoughts captive—2 Corinthians 10:5. By the way, I want you to memorize 2 Corinthians 10:5 and do what it says! Every day.

> ***"We demolish arguments and every pretension that sets itself up against the knowledge of God, and we take captive every thought to make it obedient to Christ"***
> **(2 Corinthians 10:5).**

Now, where was I? Oh, yes. Quantum computing. Before you get too freaked out, quantum computing is just a fancy way of saying "thinking." Did you know that you think faster than the speed of light? Everything you think affects every one of the cells in your body in an instant. Pretty amazing, right? Yep, God is better than a genius.

A basic definition of quantum is energy. Therefore quantum computing is "thought energy." One of my friends shared this analogy that I think fits here.

She said a car engine can run outside of a car. Not too deep, right? Just hold on, it gets a bit deeper. That running engine violently vibrates, producing immense energy, but it's of no value to the car until it's harnessed under the car's hood.

The same is with your thoughts. When you allow your thoughts to run unchecked, unharnessed, you end up nowhere useful. Until you harness the thoughts that go through your mind—which, according to communication pathologist and cognitive neuroscientist, Dr. Caroline Leaf, is estimated at six conscious bursts per second and about a million unconscious operations per second—and the management of those thoughts, you will never create new ways of handling the results of those thoughts.

In *Think, Learn, Succeed,* Dr. Caroline Leaf explains it this way.

> *"A memory is only useful if you automatize it... In order for a memory to be usable, it needs lots of energy. It gets lots of 'packets' of energy (quanta) when you repeatedly think about the memory daily..."*[23]

Did you catch that? **Repeatedly thinking about the memory energizes it to an accompanying action.** So, yeah, challenge your thinking. Be conscious of your conscious thoughts. And then apply the Scripture to capture the toxic ones and halt the detrimental behaviors that go with them.

---

23 *Think, Learn, Succeed: Understanding and Using Your Mind to Thrive at School, the Workplace, and Life* Leaf, Caroline, Baker Books, 2018.

Remember the new script! New scripts release powerful energy (quanta), which ends up transforming your mind. That is how God provides healing. He has given you a mind designed for transformation, but you decide what script you repeatedly think about until it becomes the guiding truth for your life!

I encourage you to do as I do and create multiple scripts for the different scenarios in your life. Here's a space for you to put some more of your new scripts.

Phase Three

Anything But Stuck

"Growth is painful. Change is painful. But nothing is as painful as staying stuck where you do not belong."
—N. R. Narayana Murthy

Activated Behaviors

Emotional healing comes in layers. We don't get like we are overnight, and we don't change overnight. It's like peeling the layers from an onion. Everyone wants to get to the sweet center part, but first, the outer layers need peeling away. Some tears are involved, as is patience.

The sexual assault I shared in Chapter One didn't ruin my life, but it needed to be dug up and properly buried. By avoiding the memory, I put the trauma in a shallow grave.

Now we all are probably familiar with shallow graves. I mean, hasn't everyone seen at least one episode of *CSI?* If too shallow, the smell of the dead thing rises and calls the vultures.

And that is what an old trauma is, a dead thing. It's barely covered, and every circumstance that disturbs it brings out the vultures. And we do our part to keep it stirred with our thoughts and behaviors, a.k.a. the cycle of chaos.

Now, where was I? Oh, yes, telling you "the rest of the story." God began to heal me in ways I didn't even know I needed. Nearing the end of my undergraduate year, I ran into my now-husband, Seth, at my former high school's Friday night football game. I hadn't seen Seth since the end of my senior year of high school. So, this was nearly four years later, and he was at the game watching a younger friend of his play football. Though Seth and I didn't go to high school or college together, we met in my early high school years and knew many of the same people.

About three months after running into Seth at that football game, he called me. And when I say called me—I mean left a message with my dad on a landline at my parents' house! Oh, those good ole days with house phones. To my surprise, my father left the message for me taped to my bedroom door that Seth had called for me.

I was in the middle of working my very first big girl job as a psychiatric technician at a regional hospital and finishing my undergraduate in psychology. I was also a bit lost too. Undergraduate was coming to a close, and where my future would end up was totally up in the air. I had recently moved back to my hometown and was not too excited to be there. I felt moving back home was a failure.

I wanted to avoid any pain and hurt, but I was more depressed than ever living out of state. It didn't make sense to me at the time because I am someone who is very independent and absolutely loves adventure—you would think being out of state during college would have been my jam!

However, God had other plans for me. God knew what I needed and knew I needed to run into that guy named Seth that Friday night. I eventually returned Seth's phone call and, with a severe deadly voice, quickly cut to the chase: "Why did you call me?"

I thought I was returning a phone call to him because he needed something. Like maybe he needed the phone number of one of my friends. Or needed some info on someone or to ask a quick question for which only I had the answer. I did know everything back then.

It didn't dawn on me he was calling me to get to know me. Uh, like, what is that? Thankfully that first conversation went pretty well, and it was super easy, but what relieved the pressure was that Seth was living in California. Yes! There was no pressure to date this guy—he was in California, and in the early 2000s the extent of social media was Myspace.

Well, those phone conversations became more frequent, and eventually, a few months later, he flew home, and we hung out. He wasn't going back to California. Uh, well, okay! What's going to happen now?

The truth is, Seth and I couldn't have been more different. He was one of those guys who was fun to be around, super athletic, quite nice on the eyes, but loved Jesus. Like *loved*, loved Jesus, all through his college years when everybody else was up to no good breaking those Ten Commandments with the ease of a three-year-old juggling raw eggs.

I was a disorganized, hot mess express who was one day going to get her life together but didn't have a start date for it yet. I cussed like a sailor (he tells me), but I don't remember that. Mostly, selectively.

In my naturally curious girl-who-asked-a-million-questions way, I started to know Seth. And I liked this guy because he wasn't just trying to hook up, was taking it slow getting to know me, and, bonus, was genuinely nice. I mean, I did not think this kind of man existed.

But I needed to know why he wasn't just like any of the other guys. Why was he so different? And why did he go to church on Wednesday nights and Sunday mornings, and Sunday nights? I mean, I went to church for one hour a week, tops, and that was a good and holy week for me, if it happened at all. I was like, this guy goes to church all the time. Y'all, seriously, he went to church a lot, and I went out a lot. So how did our lives even remotely cross paths? Only, God!

Thanks to all my questions, I heard Seth talk about his relationship with God and how his faith had remained steadfast through even some of the hardest years of his life. But wait—his faith got him through his hardest years. Who does that? I partied my way through my hard years. Oh, the contrast.

After a few months of talking (and apparently, me cussing), I finally dared to ask Seth, "Why don't you ever invite me to your church?" I still crack up at this because if you met some of the sweet little church ladies he went to church with, well, I probably was not who he wanted to bring to church! Picture Miss Jezebel arriving on Sunday morning to sum it up. He says that isn't so. Yeah, I told you he is a nice guy.

He said he never wanted to pressure me or make me feel that I had to attend his church. He didn't want our relationship based on that. I'm convinced he started with the basics—prayers that I would stop cussing!

So, after I practically invited myself to his church, I decided to show up for one of those Wednesday services. All you church people call them "midweek services," "Bible study groups," "youth services," "small groups"—yeah, I didn't know the church lingo. I was worried about being appropriately dressed because I didn't know if they had a "dress code." Even though I didn't understand the depths of his faith, I knew something was different, and I put it off to the outer appearance. Need I say any more?

He, of course, laughed at me and told me to wear whatever I wanted! Ummmmmm, I don't think y'all church allows that, buddy. That is the little I knew. And he, in turn, said, "Seriously, Vera, if you come on Wednesday, you better not buy a skirt just for that church service."

I, of course, bought a skirt because any reason for a new outfit was cool with me. And, yes, I got a lecture from Seth about the importance of coming as I am and just being me—not everyone else there.

Man, my outfit that night was cute, my makeup was on point, and I got wrecked in the best way possible. The mascara ended up smeared, and I forgot all about the time—something that never happened when I attended church. Did you know some people go to church for more than an hour and don't look at their watches? Crazy, I know. Now I'm not hating on the faith of my upbringing and my friends and family that I share it with—those are my people, my heart—but this was a totally new experience for me.

To hear people singing worship music to our creator and taking the time to worship God and the ultimate thing was feeling the presence of God for the first time in such a tangible way that it moved me to tears. It felt like God was hugging me, wrapping his arms around me. And the people. They prayed for me. Like right then. I had never experienced that either. I was wrecked.

Something happened inside me that night too. Bits of me, the parts that were killing me, started breaking off. The shame that had been a part of me for too long started to leave. Brokenness and unhealthy thoughts were replaced, through the Word of God and his faithful presence, with healing one shaky step at a time. Every time I attended, I became stronger and emotionally healthier. And it did take time. Years. But, with each year passing, I matured more and more in Christ and began to apply everything written in this book to my thoughts and behaviors.

Being a person who, up to this point, was a master at avoidance and various other unhealthy behaviors meant I had a deep learning curve when it came to following through on doing the hard things, not just saying I would do them. So, another big thing was activating the processes in the right manner.

As the poet Archilochus penned, *"We don't rise to the level of our expectations, we fall to the level of our training."* I'm with you, Archie!

I was a coach's daughter and spent most of my childhood at sporting events. After the games, I listened numerous times as coaches spoke about the plays, whether it was a win or a loss. I vividly remember after losses, hearing my father and his coaching buddies discuss how the plays they ran during the week before the game were not properly executed by the offense or the defense at that Friday night game. They knew what needed to happen. They practiced it repeatedly, ran through it again before the start of the game, and yet it didn't get executed as planned.

Well, to the girls reading this book that don't understand football, that means they didn't do what they were supposed to do when it really counted. When it meant the difference between winning and losing, they didn't apply what they knew when the situation called for it. As a result, their level of training didn't meet the level of execution needed.

If we want a different Chapter Two, we have to be men and women who make things happen when it counts to get a winning outcome. There will never be the perfect time other than now to activate what you have learned. We may not get it right the first time, and we may not get it right every time, but the more we work the new processes—work the cycle of success—the more we will get it right more times than we get it wrong. Until new chapter thinking becomes unconscious and begins writing itself.

Unhealthy behaviors and terrible habits get us nowhere. Just stuck, with year after year passing by in unhappy and unhealthy living. We all have an expiration date on this earth. So, make it count while you are still able. Go, make your mark on this world and start activating new behaviors toward yourself, your family, your friends, and the new people God sends in your path.

Don't get so caught up in your first chapter that you stay in a mindset of yuck and let that yuck become another reason to stay stuck. Don't stay in those negative words spoken over you or those terrible things that happened to you.

Activate the healthy, helpful actions you learned and just start taking those leaps of faith. Do something different and watch what God will do. Give him your hand, give him your will, give him the control, and watch what happens!

What does that really look like? Just like I finally opened up my big mouth and asked Seth, "Hey when are you going to invite me to your church?" I then had to actually do something different. I had to go. If I wanted a different result, I had to put myself in a new environment, I had to do something I never did before.

Early on in my career, I took a leap of faith when I applied for a job in mental health that I probably was not qualified to do. But it was something I needed. I had to take that physical step if I was ever going to push myself into the world of mental health. Was I scared? Yep. But I had to try.

Here's the thing about trying. If we are trying, we are not failing—remember that! If you are trying, you are not failing! Keep trying until your try meets up with God's will for your life.

Did I want to have a hard conversation with my biological father? Not really. That's uncomfortable. First, I changed my mindset, and then it was time to activate my behaviors. I had to open my mouth and do the hard thing.

I finally executed that play. And guess what? It wasn't a loss. It was a total win.

Maybe one day I'll write a book all about hard conversations because between my upbringing, talking to my bio father, confronting my future husband about his religion, working in mental health daily, being a business owner, and raising teenagers—I have sure learned a lot about tough conversations.

Just because conversations are tough doesn't mean the best thing to do is avoid them. Just because something is hard doesn't mean you do nothing. God had to deal with me about completing hard things. This book is one of them. Hard conversations and completing my doctorate being others. Dealing with hurt and pain and rejection and loss—it's all hard!

Here's a secret—completing the unfinished is way less difficult than the scenarios our imaginations create! And completion is rarely successful when we use our imaginations to create the script. What do I mean by that?

Remember 2 Corinthians 10:5? The part about casting down imaginations and every high thing that exalts itself against the knowledge of God? Yeah, that part. Many of our imaginations about how we think things should go because we are right and those people who hurt us are wrong—yes, those thoughts—exalt themselves above what God knows. What do we do then?

Well, we seek God and find out when and how we should complete the hard conversations and in which manner. We find out God's will for our lives and his priority—not our priorities.

You see, one of my top priorities was getting as much education as I possibly could in my field. The highest academic level. Running myself ragged yet again. I felt I had sought God to pursue my last and final degree—my doctorate in counseling.

I talked to my husband, and he and I went back and forth and back and forth. He didn't really want me to do it—yes, he is still that nice guy, but he knows me better than anyone else on this earth. He knew I already had a lot of irons in the fire and at the point I started the doctorate program, I was already my own boss and a licensed therapist.

Seth just didn't feel it was necessary. I was already experiencing a significant amount of success. I recall very clearly him saying, "Vera, are you really going to give yourself a pay raise just because you get called Dr. Vera now?" Ha! He had a point.

I was self-employed already and wasn't giving myself a pay raise unless the Lord opened more financial doors. And for me, that was not a top priority. I know for some, money is a big motivator. But for me being happy and helping people is enough by itself. So, I definitely wasn't pursuing a doctorate for a pay raise.

It was a personal thing for me. Over the years, I had finally proven myself in the mental health world, and I always secretly struggled with the negative belief that I was not smart. That I didn't have the intelligence to be at that level. Crazy how we sell ourselves short. But I believed that so many others were much more intelligent than I and that I just couldn't compete on that level.

The fear of failure and not being enough haunted me. After getting my master's degree, I had finally broken out of that mindset about schooling. I knew I was capable, and I was motivated. You take a motivated Southern girl, and baby, you better watch out! She does not have to be the smartest woman in the room, but if she is motivated to work, she will outwork anyone! That was me. I was going to work and work and work and show the world I could do it!

And boy did I. Until I just couldn't go anymore. The university I was attending for my doctorate school made some changes, which meant my dissertation work would have to be changed a bit. More edits. More research. Back to the drawing board. Oh, my goodness, no. My mind couldn't handle it. So, I stopped. Then I avoided it. And then I cried. And then I pushed it to the back of my mind and said, "I am not thinking about this anymore! I quit!"

I wasn't someone who quit school or anything else for that matter. I am someone who performs well under pressure. I also really love a good challenge, and someone telling me I can't do something looks a lot like a challenge!

Entertaining thoughts of quitting when I was so close to defending my dissertation work just threw me into a tailspin. In my brokenness, I went to the Lord, and he reminded me that I was yet again taking something and making it Vera's, not his. I had taken the driver's seat and driven off the path God had for me. I was so busy that I didn't consult with God about my dissertation—to talk to him about "boring" research.

Instead, God allowed another meltdown, and during this meltdown, I humbled myself and started writing what he originally put on my heart. The thing he originally put on my heart was *Beauty From Ashes.* The curriculum for women. This book. This type of work. Not dissertation research for a doctoral degree.

As the *Beauty From Ashes* classes took off, God spoke to me so clearly and reminded me that he was equipping me, and no psychology book could ever do that! The greatest psychology book ever written is the Word of God, and it is absolutely and entirely enough.

God told me to close the chapter of my dissertation work and just be obedient to him. And he didn't tell me at that time if I would ever circle back and finally complete what I was so close to finishing. And I had really good grades.

But you know what? That didn't matter. That wasn't the lesson God was trying to teach me. Who cares about grades? Well, that would be me, Vera Holloway. I care. God said, "Once again, your priorities do not align with mine, my girl!"

Do you know what happened? God sent one person after another to a *Beauty From Ashes* course to my office to teach me something more. To write a little something more. To comfort me a little more in knowing that my choice to be obedient to him and answer his call was more important.

One day in prayer, I cried out to God, and he brought to my mind Isaiah chapter 61. I immediately grabbed my Bible and went there. I realized that part of my Bible was already highlighted and marked. And I had written a date on that passage of Scripture. I read where I wrote, *Your ministry* beside that Scripture. I reread those words, *Your ministry.*

God has a reminder for you too. Are you looking for it?

Phase Four
Healthy Boundaries

"You get what you tolerate."
— Dr. Henry Cloud

"The boundary lines have fallen for me in pleasant places; surely I have a delightful inheritance" (Psalm 16:6).

Boundaries

Just as our homes have physical property lines and neighbors, friends and strangers are not allowed to hang out uninvited, we also have personal property lines too. Problems happen when we either have too lax boundaries, have no boundaries causing us to be abused or taken advantage of, or our boundaries are too rigid to invite relationships.

What are personal boundaries? Personal boundaries are the limits we create for what we accept as reasonable, safe, and permissible behavior from others toward us. These boundaries also define our responses when someone exceeds the limits we have in place.

A lack of boundaries or inability to stick to boundary settings is rooted in fear—fear of loss, retaliation, or the guilt of saying no. Loss may look like a relationship we want to keep or a measure of respect we think we have with someone who will leave us abandoned, alone, or without provision. Retaliation in the form of passive-aggressive responses, untrue tales told to others about our "hard-heartedness," or possibly the loss of a job if we enforce a boundary violated by a superior at our workplace.

Regardless of the source of our fear, it's vital to our mental and emotional health that we set boundaries and enforce them. And by enforcing them I'm not talking about a boundary set with prison-grade razor wire, I'm talking about an invisible line that, by consistency, people know what we will and won't tolerate.

What determines our boundaries? Our beliefs, opinions, attitudes, past history, and social encounters and their outcomes—whether positive or negative—determine our boundaries or lack thereof.

Are you seeing how unhealthy "family rules" and traumatic experiences from childhood can fail to give you a system for creating healthy boundaries? Don't look at this as hopeless or an indictment of your upbringing. View it instead as an observation, an ah-ha moment.

One of the best-known personalities on boundaries,[24] psychologist and best-selling author, Dr. Henry Cloud, states that if you have an internal conflict, you have a boundary conflict. That's fairly straightforward, right? He advises you to check your love (the relationships in your life) and limits (the boundaries you have set with these relationships) as those two areas may conflict.

Good relationships learn how to handle the *no's* we give them. Boundaries are not dependent on others and how well they honor our boundaries. Boundaries are dependent on us. We are responsible for our boundaries and are the maintainers of them. So, keep your fences mended!

24 https://www.drcloud.com/

Where Are Your Lines with Self?

Feelings
Attitudes
Behavior
Choices
Limits
Thoughts
Talents
Desires

Where Are Your Lines with Others?

Spouse/Partner
Children (minor age and adult)
Family Members
Church/Ministry
Friendships

People need structure. We were created for it. Love also needs structure; it needs to say *no*. Our lives should be a series of limits. Yes, no, Yes, no, Yes, no—you get the picture.

Do you know what healthy boundaries look like? If not, let me help you out.

Game Plan for Boundary Setting:

1. Identify your fears one at a time. If you can't rightly identify the fear, keep asking yourself the *what* question. "What am I afraid of?" "What is the root of this?" Get God involved in the asking and identifying process.
2. Take responsibility for your behaviors and role in not sticking with solid boundaries in the past. Own where you have tolerated things you should not have. Just because you have tolerated something in the past does not mean you have to continue. Another bad decision does not fix a bad decision. Learning and growing do not make us hypocrites, they make us wise.
3. Understand you need more than just willpower. You can't do this without Jesus. Living a self-disciplined life means you develop new healthy habits and stay consistent with them. Give yourself some kindness—developing new habits takes time.
4. Open up to outside sources. People you trust who cheer you on and motivate you are a must-have. Look for people who are emotionally intelligent and who also operate in the wisdom that comes from God. You want people who can teach you, pray with you, support you, and give you honest feedback.

5. Understand planned consequences and natural consequences. Stop protecting others from consequences while you bear the burden of their choices. Remember, the majority of our consequences come from our personal choices.

Phase Five
Healthy Emotions

"Gratitude, like faith, is a muscle. The more you use it, the stronger it grows." — Alan Cohen

"The Spirit of the Sovereign Lord is on me, because the Lord has anointed me to proclaim good news to the poor.

He has sent me to bind up the brokenhearted, to proclaim freedom for the captives and release from darkness for the prisoners, to proclaim the year of the Lord 's favor and the day of vengeance of our God, to comfort all who mourn, and provide for those who grieve in Zion— ***to bestow on them a crown of beauty instead of ashes, the oil of joy instead of mourning, and a garment of praise instead of a spirit of despair.***

They will be called oaks of righteousness, a planting of the Lord for the display of his splendor"

(Isaiah 61:1–3).

The emphasis on the Scripture above is mine, but the promise it declares to you is from God.

Practicing thanksgiving every day will balance your emotions like nothing else ever will. Ask God to help you to only put on the garments your present situation needs. Nothing more, nothing less. God won't let you down.

Now it's time to take a gratitude inventory. Get creative. Throw in some art with it.

I am thankful for

Phase Six

Secure Attachments

Your Second Chapter

"Nothing can bring a real sense of security into the home except true love."
— Billy Graham

In Chapter One, Phase Four, I discussed what unhealthy attachment styles look like and how from birth attachment styles depend on our caregivers. We didn't get to decide how we attach, our first chapter was already written for us. But we get to write our second chapter (congrats because you have already started yours)!

What do secure attachments look like? Secure people form secure attachments. Insecure people form insecure attachments. Secure people are content, grateful, social, warm, empathic, easy to connect with, able to express their feelings, and able to build and maintain deep and lasting relationships with others. They are well liked in social settings and in the workplace.

No, this doesn't mean you have to be a social butterfly to be a secure person. It just simply means that when you are around others, you have the ability to make them feel secure all while not feeling insecure yourself.

How do you get to a place of secure attachments with yourself and others? Here are a few easy questions to ask yourself and apply to every season of your life.

Whether it's with raising your children or transitioning to supporting that now-grown child, connecting with friends, improving your current relationships, taking on a new job, or just working on breaking free from codependency and insecure attachments, these questions will help you evaluate, adjust, and grow. I created a self-inventory for evaluating personal secure attachment. I use it myself as well as with my clients. Now it's yours too.

1. Safety
   - Do I feel safe?
   - Does my child feel safe?
   - Does my partner feel safe with me?

2. Seen and Known
   - Do I feel seen and known?
   - Does my child feel seen and really known by me?
   - Does my partner feel seen and really known by me?

3. Comfort and Reassurance
   - Do I feel comfort and reassurance?
   - Does my child feel comfort and reassurance from me?
   - Does my partner feel comfort and reassurance from me?

4. Value
   - Do I feel valued?
   - Does my child feel valued by me?
   - Does my partner feel valued by me?

5. Encouraged to Explore
    - Do I feel supported to explore?
    - Does my child feel supported and encouraged to explore?
    - Does my partner feel supported and encouraged to explore?

Take some time to answer these questions personally and ask the people closest to you if you are doing the above for them. Take the time to actually listen to them. Don't try to change their opinions or answers. Let them truly respond to you and then journal their responses.

If one area is not the answer you like, don't get caught in the cycle of chaos with negative thought patterns, behaviors, and emotions. If their honest answer provides you with sadness, process the sadness, own it, and remember its purpose. Now take what they have told you and use it as your catalyst for change.

As a therapist, I often ask my children or husband some of these questions. I'll tell you truthfully, I went into these questions thinking they would respond better than they did! I mean—how dare they? But, over the years I had to change that script and really learn that the people closest to me really saw something that I didn't always see. I had blind spots they saw clearly. These hard questions and sometimes hard responses made me a better person. But, the better me didn't happen until I was ready to get out of my own way by leaving my Chapter One. After I learned what needed to improve, I had to activate the change.

I can remember a time when my husband felt I didn't value and appreciate him. I was so busy climbing the "corporate ladder," getting all the education, proving myself as a businesswoman, and taking care of the kids' needs that he felt totally neglected.

Our daughter was diagnosed in her early elementary school years with dyslexia and ADHD. Every extra moment I had in the afternoons was used making sure she had what she needed. Those early years were tough because I wanted her to have everything she needed to be successful.

Hearing my husband say he felt unappreciated, taken for granted, and not valued just crushed me. I spiraled into a victim mentality cycle of chaos. Well, that changed nothing! And it kept us at a stuck place in our marriage.

I thought he was critical and didn't see how hard I worked and how much I poured out toward my children and in the workplace. But what I was failing to see was that I wasn't providing him a secure attachment.

Once I learned what he needed, then it was my responsibility to activate those behaviors that provided for those needs. I set new boundaries and learned a new balance because at the end of the day saving the world is not more important than taking care of what was given to me first—my husband and my children.

One of my most favorite quotes that I probably need to have made into a wall plaque is by Mother Theresa. She said, *"If you want to change the world, go home and love your family."*

Start with what has been given to you—those in front of you: your family, your friends, if you have a spouse, if you have children. Do this inventory and then get to work on how you can make the most important people in your life feel secure.

And lastly, most importantly, work on making yourself feel secure too.

Phase Seven

Cycle of Success

"Success is not final, failure is not fatal: it is the courage to continue that counts." — Winston S. Churchill

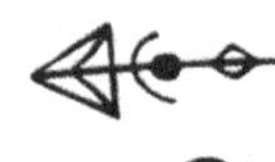

People-pleasing – I need to say no because my schedule is full

1. "Vera, you have a family, a counseling practice, a business with five locations – three of which are now lost to a hurricane, so you have to find new locations and get up and running, and you are on a book deadline. What will people say if I turn them down? I have the skills to help; why wouldn't I help? I always help."

2. I take a mental step back and allow "but" to enter the thought cycle. "I want to, but if I want to remain sane and healthy, I have to say no. Saying no is not negative. Saying no sets boundaries that help complete the goals that I have already given a yes. Saying no helps me stay in my lane. I will graciously say no."

3. Saying no helped me keep my family first. I was able to complete this book on time. I gave it my full attention and enjoyed writing and doing what I needed to do instead of something I wasn't supposed to do.

4. My feelings are relief, joy, satisfaction that I chose balance and purpose over accommodation that would have left me in a chaotic place.

Your turn to fill in a cycle of success.

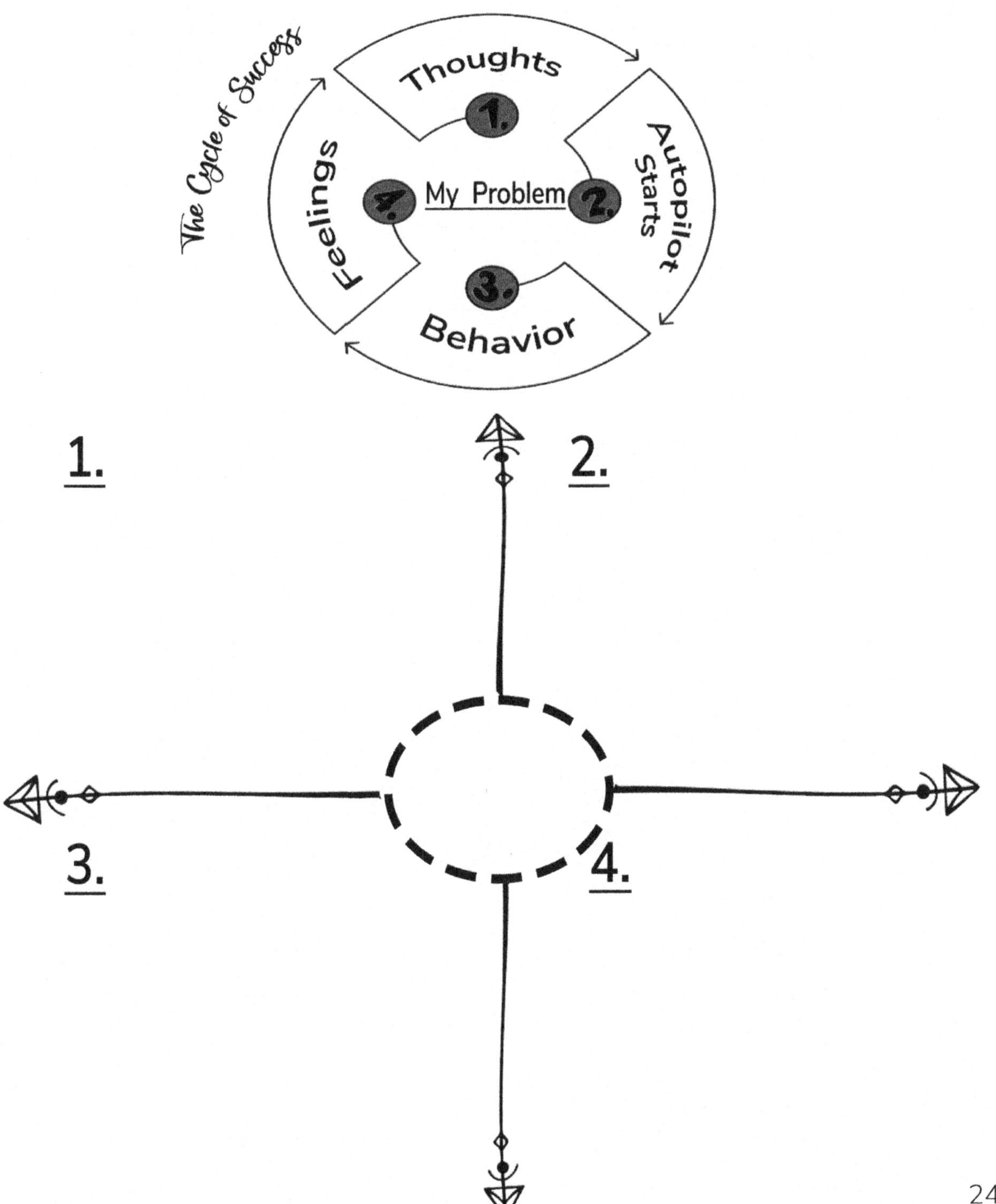

Phase Eight

Forgiveness & Self-Love

"Forgiveness is an act of the will, and the will can function regardless of the temperature of the heart."
— Corrie Ten Boom

On forgiving ourselves, I heard someone say that when we withhold forgiveness of ourselves, we stand in place of God. Why would we want to remove God's forgiveness and replace it with our judgment? Are we greater than God? I think self-flagellation keeps many of us caught in a cycle of chaos. It's no news to God that we don't deserve heaven. Maybe we need to stop rejecting his forgiveness with our self-contempt. It's something to think about.

Forgiveness. I love what my first pastor, Bishop Ronnie Melancon, says about forgiveness. He says that forgiveness is for—giving—it to God. It's our responsibility to give it to God, and then God handles the rest. Forgiveness is never just for the other person. Forgiveness is for us. It's a necessary step. You may also need to forgive yourself.

Sadly, many of us will never get the apology we always wished or hoped to receive. In my personal story, I was able to have closure with my biological father. I was also able to continue on a very healthy path of healing with my mom and dad. And I was able to experience great healing in my marriage, although it started very rocky.

God restored. God is still restoring. He is still teaching me and giving me opportunities to reach across the wall to people of other backgrounds, other religions, and other walks and be the hands and feet of Jesus.

But what doesn't sit well with me is that many of my clients and friends wouldn't be able to hear, "I am sorry. I wronged you."

Sometimes, due to death, we will never hear those words. Sometimes, due to the necessary boundaries we have in place, having a healing conversation will never be an option. There are so many variables why we may never hear, "I am sorry."

I went to God, and I asked him if there was anything I could do to help those who would never get that apology. I wanted to give you something. I wanted to make sure you knew your Father loved you.

God's response got me writing. I began writing the words I knew so many of my clients wished they could have heard. So, I wrote for them. I wrote it for you. I wrote it to be shared.

Beauty From Ashes. Trade your ash and watch what he will do.

I didn't see you; I didn't really know you, I didn't know your heart and desires because I was selfish and stuck in my own world. I am sorry.

Today I give you what the Word of God says, *"Delight yourself in the Lord and he will give you the desires of your heart."* For I failed you, but God will never fail you. (Psalm 37:4)

I inflicted pain on you when I physically abused you. I embarrassed you and caused you much shame and for that I am sorry.

Today I impart Isaiah 61:7 over your life: *"Instead of shame and dishonor you will enjoy a double share of honor. You will possess a double portion of prosperity in your land, and everlasting joy will be yours."*

I inflicted shame on you when I violated your body. I never had a right to touch you in the manner in which I did, but I still did it. I am sorry for putting my selfish desires and urges before you.

But today I speak the Word of God over your life: *"to proclaim the year of the Lord's favor and the day of vengeance of our God, to comfort all who mourn, and provide for those who grieve in Zion—to bestow on them a crown of beauty instead of ashes"* (Isaiah 61:1–3).

I am sorry for taking away your security and making you feel insecure.

But today I remind you that your soul can find rest in God alone. It is only through him that you can find salvation. He is your rock and your fortress and he will never be shaken. (Psalm 62:1–2)

I am sorry that I allowed my pain to inflict the same pain on you.

But I bring you the Scripture of Romans 8:31: *"If God is for us, who can be against us?"* God is for you. Hand him over the pain once and for all because he is ready to fight for you!

I am sorry I was not the father you needed. I was absent. I am sorry that I wasn't the mother you needed. I didn't fight for you when you were wronged. I didn't advocate for you, I didn't put your emotional, physical, and spiritual needs first. I choose me, my feelings, and how others would view me before fighting for you. For that I am sorry.

The Word of God promises us that when your mother or father forsakes you, the Lord will receive you. He will teach you his ways and lead you to the straight path. I failed to lead you correctly, but the Lord will always guide you correctly. (Psalm 27:10)

I am sorry for stealing your self-confidence. I sent the message in many ways that you were not enough. But that was a lie.

You are a child of God. The King of Kings is who you belong to. The daughters and sons of the most high. Christ's friend. He chooses you. You are the salt and light of the earth. (John 1:12, John 15:15, Matthew 5:13–14)

I am sorry for threatening you to keep your abuse a secret. I was only protecting myself.

But I say to you today, don't be afraid of your past, for the Word of God says, *"For the time is coming when everything that is covered will be revealed, and all that is secret will be made known to all"* (Matthew 10:26).

I am sorry for making you steal, lie, and manipulate others.

But today I proclaim over your life that you may approach God with freedom and confidence. That cannot be stolen from you! (Ephesians 3:12)

I am sorry that you had to constantly move, and I chose my way of life over your stability.

But be reassured that all things work together for good and what the enemy has meant to destroy you cannot and will not! (Romans 8:28)

I am sorry for stealing your childhood, your physical safety, and your emotional stability.

But be reassured that you can do all things through Christ who gives you strength. Your childhood may have been stolen, but today you are given strength through the Word of God and the power of his Holy Spirit. (Philippians 4:13)

I am sorry for lashing out in pain and making you fear me.

But today I impart God's Word to you: *"Do not fear, for I am with you; do not be dismayed, for I am your God. I will strengthen you and help you; I will uphold you with my righteous right hand"* (Isaiah 41:10).

I am sorry for always being in control and not trusting God to guide me. I was only trusting myself and my own abilities and for that I was wrong.

Today I declare the Word of God over your life which says to: *"Trust in the Lord with all your heart and lean not on your own understanding and in all your ways submit to him and he will make your path straight"* (Proverbs 3:5–6).

I am sorry I made you ashamed of my behaviors and I embarrassed you. I am sorry you began to behave in the same ways I did.

But today I proclaim God's Word over you that when you gave your life to Christ your old ways are now "hidden with Christ in God." *"So, put to death whatever belongs to your earthly nature: sexual immorality, impurity, lust, evil desires and greed, which is idolatry. You used to walk in these ways, in the life you once lived. But now you must rid yourself of all such things as these: anger, rage, malice, slander, and filthy language from your lips"* (Colossians 3:2–8).

I am sorry I didn't have a true relationship with God and therefore you were never shown what a true Christian household was like.

But today you have the choice to allow God to save you and your household. The decision is up to you, but it is one decision that can change the rest of your life. (Acts 16:31)

I am sorry I was a womanizer and choose sex before my family's needs. For this I am sorry.

As the Word of God says: *"Nothing in all creation is hidden from God's sight. Everything is uncovered and laid bare before the eyes of him to whom we must give account."* For these sins were sins of your family and you have the power to break free of that generational pattern once and for all. (Hebrews 4:13)

I am sorry I brought many men into the home while you were growing up. Because of my actions you have been unable to develop healthy relationships with men. I am sorry for this.

Today, I declare the spirit of fear to be broken in your life and I release peace that passes all understanding, self-control, and wisdom to understand when and when not to enter a relationship. (Philippians 4:7)

Today and moving forward, let these apologies turn into your greatest praise and proclaim the promises that the Word of God has for you.

It's time. You are faithful and trustworthy to your Father in heaven, and he loves to reward his children. Your battle is won. Great is God's faithfulness. Peace is your inheritance.

I want you to think of an apology you have never gotten or maybe reference back to what I have written above. What did you need to hear? I want you to write it down. After writing it down, I want you to read it out loud. I want you to believe that you are worthy of that apology. If you are still struggling, I want you to reread out loud some of the apologies that I have written along with the prayer and Scriptures that replace the pain. Sometimes we have to read out loud something over and over until it becomes a habitual thought. Remember that lesson? Yes, of course, you do. You are an amazing student.

Phase Nine

Your Chapter Two

***"Take the first step in faith.
You don't have to see the whole staircase,
just take the first step."
— Martin Luther King Jr.***

Think it.

Write it.

Believe it.

Activate it.

We don't do what we don't believe.

This is your page, don't waste it.

Acknowledgements

First, let me say this may be the longest acknowledgement of all the acknowledgements ever to acknowledge those that need acknowledging. But since I had an emotional breakdown after writing the last word of this book if this bothers you, just skip over it.

To even find the proper words to express my gratitude seems so very difficult. The completion of this book would not have taken place had it not been for the people below. They are hands down the reason you are reading this today.

God - My way-maker. My miracle worker. My promise keeper. That is who you are. My first father. My comforter and almighty counselor. The words in this book mean nothing without you. You give the power and the increase. I will forever worship you and call you savior. Saying "thank you" will never be enough. I will just keep moving out of the way and let you lead because your plans are much cooler than mine! You are much more creative and adventurous than my wildest dreams - so I'll just keep submitting to your will.

Seth - I just cry when I start to write a note of thanksgiving to you. I want the perfect words for you, but since I just wrote a book about breaking out of such thinking, I'll refrain! Truth is you do deserve the perfect words. After God, you are my tough yet loving counselor, confidant, and the spiritual leader of our home. You are steadfast and faithful and yet you chose hot mess express me all those years ago. What you saw in my mess is still a mystery to me, but thanks for so passionately loving me and being so faithful to making our marriage, children, ministry, and businesses successful. There isn't a day that goes by that I question if I am loved - I know I am. You activate your love for me every day. I see it when you take a deep breath and smile - after I tell you another crazy idea I have, or some crazy emotion I am feeling in the moment, or when I am redecorating the house at 2am. You have allowed me to take risks and you have supported me through the good and the bad. The ups and the downs. You still remain. I will forever be in awe of your love for me, and I'll keep working every day to make sure you know that you are loved, valued, and respected. Thank you for allowing me to share my heart with others, whether it's in the counseling chair or spending hours writing a book. You give up time with me, so that I can help others. Truly selfless. I love you with everything in me and I can't thank you enough.

Jacques & Juliette - To the greatest miracles (besides your dad) with which God has blessed me. Being your mom is more than an honor. It's my greatest ministry on this earth. Jacques I am blown away by your maturity, dedication, and love for God. Thank you for always being so kind to me (for a teenager, this is impressive) and looking out for your momma! To hear you talk about me in a positive and loving way is one of the most humbling things. Seriously, I am convinced you are the nicest kid out there! Please never change. You possess so many qualities of your father and it's a blessing to watch it unfold. I love having a front row seat and watching you mature into quite the man! Thank you for being so patient with me during this process of writing a book and understanding just how important it is to answer the call God has placed on my heart.

To my Juju girl! My Juliette Marie who is a mini me. God bless you. And God bless your Papa with the grace and mercy to handle a mini-Vera. And Jacques as well because we can both give them a run for their money! Your heart and the way you love people is just amazing to see. The way you love me, encourage me, and give constant hugs and kisses is just the sweetest around! Juju you are a mighty little prayer warrior and to see you already answering that call is beautiful. I have no doubt God will use every creative talent and gift he has given you if you just continue to yield to his will. Thank you for sharing your momma! Even though you don't ever want me to be gone from the house or work late, you are so sweet to always find out what's going on and how the book is going.

Jacques and Juju - I love you both with all of me!

Chermaine - To my spiritual momma, editor, confidant, and mentor — thank you is just not enough. You have made sure this project got completed. You believed in me when I didn't believe in myself. You gave me deadlines and structure that I, oh, so needed! You have a gift for making me feel so smart by simply tweaking my words a bit! My only regret is that I didn't know you in high school and college. I sure could have used this amazing gift of editing and collaborative writing that you have graciously given! I know this is your job to edit, but you are so much more than an editor. You are walking in your calling and truly doing the Lord's work! I am excited to see what's in store for you and The People Company!

Mom - To the sweetest woman on the bayou! You have a servant's heart, and, for my entire life, you have given of yourself so selflessly. You are always a helping hand in a time of need. Whether that is helping me with the kids, washing or ironing my family's clothes (just so I can actually get caught up), or running errands for me — your answer is always yes! Spoiled me a bit much? Ummm, yeah you did that! Thank you for never given up on that strong independent girl who was going to do things her way! You so patiently and graciously loved me through it all. Even when we both felt hurt - we still chose to love! You are a testament to my kindness and patience with people. I got it from my momma!

Dad - From day one of meeting you, I was asking you tough questions! Do you remember the first tough question I asked you after meeting you for the very first time? "Are you going to be my new daddy?" Tearjerker from the beginning. I have no doubt been taking you on a roller coaster ride from the start and I guess that's never stopped. You have been a constant in my life since I was a little girl. You chose me. You didn't have too, but you did. I have never felt anything else but yours. Although, moments of our relationship were painful and the start to my second chapter found you absent, you caught up and have been there every day since. Thank you for being there and being a wonderful support to me, Seth, Jacques, and Juliette.

The Holloway's - Thank you to my amazing in laws! You guys have loved me from day one and I have truly been humbled by your generosity and affection. You have created amazing children and quite a legacy for your family. All of your children, their spouses, and grandchildren serve the Lord! All because of one decision you made that changed the course of your generation and has now led to future generations being blessed! Thank you. Our life is better because of your decisions, your wisdom, and your guidance. To my sister-in-law and brothers-in-law - you guys rock and are such a blessing to me.

The Biondini Family - My originals from day one! Thank you for loving me and accepting me, my sister, my mom, and all of my extended family so well. We could all write a book on how to do blended families well. Thank you for allowing us to be a part of the Austrian & Italian way of life. I have so many wonderful memories because of you all. Your love and support have truly helped me to write that second chapter.

Alli Worthington - You guide me week after week. Your coaching, experience, and support are a blessing to me. From the start of this book through completion of it and now promotion - your knowledge is invaluable. Thank you for your energy and your continued deadlines. I have truly needed it. From one Enneagram seven to another - thank you for just getting me!

House of Prayer - From the pastoral staff to the members of House of Prayer - you all have made my life better in the best possible way. From the first day I walked through the doors and still today, you make me feel nothing but loved. My greatest spiritual moments have been at the altars of House of Prayer. I am thankful for a place that focuses first on prayer and then on loving people. I have felt your prayers, loved your guidance and correction, and the constant stability you bring to my life.

Pastors Josh & Keesha - You two have been constants in my family's life. It's an honor to do ministry alongside you. I am thankful for your support and guidance. I respect just how hard of a job you two have. Your commitment and dedication are not something I take lightly. Thank you for your leadership, guidance, and support to not just myself but my husband, children, and extended family.

The People Company - Thank you for taking a chance on me. You didn't have to, but you did! It's been such a blessing in my life to collaborate with like-minded believers. Thank you for lending me Cher for the last year! She is the reason publications will happen with girls like me. She keeps her clients in line. I love it.

First BFA Class & Cross Church - Thank you, Pastors Rachelle and Brandon, for being the first to give me a place to share my heart and original curriculum with the women of your church. I haven't forgotten your kindness, words of encouragement, and love. Thank you to my first BFA class and my sister law, Mandy, who would join each week! Your vulnerability in sharing your stories taught me so much. It is because of this very first class I am even in this place today. So, thanks for taking a chance on me and attending week after week. I will always remember you with gratitude.

The BFA Students (that followed that original group) - I have met so many amazing women through this curriculum since it launched. The fact that you showed up each week and grew in your relationship with the Lord while also working on your healing journey was remarkable and beyond brave. You chose to team up with other women - love them, support them, encourage them - and you also shared your story in that process. You are another reason this book was possible.

My Clients: You trust me with your vulnerability and allow me to walk alongside you. You teach me more than any graduate school program ever could. It humbles me, and I am honored at the invitation into your world. Thank you.

When your Chapter Two has been written, I want to hear about it. Share it with me by connecting at www.veraholloway.com or my private Facebook group for *Your Second Chapter* book.

XO,

Vera

Made in the USA
Coppell, TX
28 June 2022